The Educated Underclass

The Educated Underclass

Students and the Promise of Social Mobility

Gary Roth

PLUTO PRESS

First published 2019 by Pluto Press
345 Archway Road, London N6 5AA

www.plutobooks.com

British Library Cataloguing in Publication Data
A catalogue record for this book is available from the British Library

ISBN   978 0 7453 3923 8   Hardback
ISBN   978 0 7453 3922 1   Paperback
ISBN   978 1 7868 0441 9   PDF eBook
ISBN   978 1 7868 0443 3   Kindle eBook
ISBN   978 1 7868 0442 6   EPUB eBook

Typeset by Stanford DTP Services, Northampton, England

Simultaneously printed in the United Kingdom and United States of America

Contents

Figures and tables

Figures

Tables

Acknowledgments

Because this project was so long in the imagination, it owes thanks to many people, including Richard Seltzer, Susan Carruthers, Grace Roosevelt, Jules Bartkowski, Fran Bartkowski, Peter Sieger, Clay Hartjen, Barbara Foley, Carolyne White, and Matias Scaglione, all of whom listened and responded at key moments. From the Department of Sociology at Rutgers-Newark, my appreciation to Sherri-Ann Butterfield, Genese Sodikoff, Jamie Lew, and Chris Duncan for their support. Also to Anna Austenfeld for her expertise with the graphics and David Shulman from Pluto Press for shepherding this along.

Former students spoke to me in depth about their upbringings, parental understandings of education and class, and their experiences on the job market. Their openness and keen insights find expression throughout the text: Stephanie Avila, Stephanie Blissett, Maurice Chambers, Kaneesha Helms, Daniel Hernandez, Maisem Jaloudi, Bianca Lesende, Ashley Pennington, Ghada Saleh, Letisha Springer, and Alicia Vega.

Paul Mattick encouraged me to write about education by opening *The Brooklyn Rail* to my first forays into the field. Some passages are incorporated into what follows. He also urged me to keep rewriting until this version finally appeared.

Julie Shiroishi helped me untangle a draft that had left me also in knots. She possesses an unusual gift for clarity.

To Anne Lopes, who continues to push against a system for any openings it might provide on behalf of students.

Preface

For many years I experienced up close the byways of the collegiate system, at first as a student at a mid-sized residential college, then as a college dropout, and finally as a slightly older returning student at a large public university. It was a meandering and often frustrating journey, but it was within this world that I would eventually make my career. An in-service teacher education program and a doctorate overseas rounded out my student experiences.

What followed was a stint as a full-time adjunct (teaching the same course thirteen times in two-and-a-half years) and a position as the director of a for-profit school that trained "ability-to-benefit" students (for example, high school dropouts) for entry-level word processing and data entry jobs. I had traversed the educational continuum, even though this had not been my intention.

A series of positions within the academic affairs arena of an urban public research institution came next. This always entailed pushing against rigid rules and the lack of institutional response to the needs of students. To have any impact required an effort that began in the forty-first hour, such were the week-to-week demands of administration. Politically, I viewed this as being a "good social democrat," about as much as anyone could hope to achieve within the confines of the existing educational system. Without a strong a priori commitment, even this was utopian.

For the last several years I have taught full-time, a sort of "golden parachute" for senior administrators with lengthy terms of service. This has given me an opportunity to express ideas more fully and more openly than before. But how to do so with undergraduates has been an ongoing puzzle, since they present their own unique complications as learners.

Mass education, rather than elite instruction, has been my motivator. A special challenge is represented by the attempt to extract the best teaching and pedagogic practices that have been distilled at small liberal arts institutions and then adapt them for a diverse, urban, and often undereducated student body. What does one mean, for instance, by faculty-student interaction when sixty students sit in the classroom?

My students live in a world quite familiar to me. My family, a product of the post-World War II baby boom, rarely if ever mentioned class. Religion was the more relevant discussion, a result of an "inter-marriage" that my father's extended family could not accept. This was a source of keen resentment for my parents, even though neither was particularly devout. Class, however, might have been just as intense a focal point.

As a child during the 1930s Great Depression, my mother was proletarian through-and-through. It was a time of deep unhappiness for her. Her father, already reduced from the ranks of a silversmith to that of an ad hoc refuse collector, was removed from the household because of tuberculosis. The sanitarium was three hours distant, a bus ride with multiple connections. Throughout her adolescence, a few odd family visits dotted his last five years. Family lore held that if my mother had grown up wealthy, a full-fledged medical career might have been possible, rather than employment as a high school-educated lab technician. It was a question of intelligence, but without the requisite education.

My father's story was much more complicated. His father, an immigrant, worked in sweatshops and attended night school in order to complete his secondary education. Because he was literate and male, he held a position as a supervisor and served as a shop steward. Advanced training as a pharmacist followed. My father's brothers were both college-educated, one also as a pharmacist, the other gained his Ph.D. in physics and built missiles for a career. My father, though, was a high school dropout, a life-determining decision made halfway through adolescence. At age fifteen, he falsified his birth certificate and joined the merchant marine.

About my grandmothers, nothing was ever said, either in terms of education or occupations. But whereas non-working wives were once taken as signs of a family's success, over the last half-century such situations became exclusive markers for either the very wealthy or the abjectly poor.

My parents spent the post-war decades, my childhood, clawing their way into what they considered the middle class. In truth, my parents were part of a bifurcated working class that emerged during the second half of the twentieth century, convinced that advanced education was the means for their children to exit a fate that they had not succeeded in escaping. The focus on education almost seemed to cleave the working population into two discrete groups. For my students too, "working class" is not a self-description freely chosen.

For these reasons, the relationship between education and class has been a long-standing interest for me.

Introduction

This is a book about class, and also about the division of the populace into distinct strata. I use college students as my entrée into these themes, since this is the part of the population with which I am so familiar. Most people, including my students, identify themselves as part of a vast middle class, to which virtually everybody, they claim, belongs. It is an understanding of class based on occupations, income, places of residence, consumerism, and education. Otherwise, there are just the rich and the poor, not really social classes as much as clusters of the fortunate and unfortunate. As one student explained: "until I came to college, I had never heard of the working class. There were only the lower, middle, and upper classes."

When spoken to about class, or asked to probe its deeper significance, these students have a great deal to say, but left on their own, the discourse of class is not one in which they engage. It is easy to spot students whose previous coursework focused on such issues. They discuss the working class without hesitation, as if their education has already made them upwardly mobile.

To talk about class is part of the process of moving beyond it. It's why students from elite backgrounds speak about class so effortlessly, having grown up with a terminology that is pervasive throughout the upper orders of society. The discussion of class presupposes a wide view of social affairs, one that is directed outward and beyond. To speak about class without rancor is to speak from a distance, itself a measure of privilege.

Nonetheless, few people outside the classroom still mention the working class except in negative terms. It is a terminology that dates to the not-so-distant past. It is also a terminology that has taken on an antiquarian tone, despite its continued use. "Working people" is a common alternative. "Working poor" is popular within journalism and policy discussions. In politics, "working Americans" has become a universal descriptor. In everyday parlance, though, the middle class is the new working class. The working class per se has morphed into a remnant of a dysfunctional capitalism.

Education and class

Class is relational, representing a position of dependency on a social system that works according to its own logic, not to that of the people who serve it. "Wealth", Paul Mattick writes, "appears to be a matter of commodity ownership, or the possession of money, a means to ownership, rather than a relationship between people manifested in differential access to goods."[1]

Material things separate people and make them unequal economically, people who otherwise are uniquely diverse in their individuality and who also share a similar fate vis-à-vis society at large. A focus on class emphasizes those aspects of social reality that people have in common, such as the dependence on employment and laboring activity, whereas difference and differences are stressed by the social sciences.

How to understand the role of education within these two realms of equality and inequality is the task I have set for *The Educated Underclass*. On the one side is the everyday world of commodities, money, possessions, and income inequality; on the other, a broader domain that evokes a status that is society-wide and absolute. Fitting these two realities together is not a simple matter. The working population, for instance, tends to downplay its importance within the productive chain in order to focus on rewards promised to it in the sphere of income and consumption.

Because my starting point is experienced reality, albeit viewed with a critical eye, I use some of the same terminology and ways of examining social relations as the people I am investigating. It is my intention, nonetheless, to also show that a huge working class is reemerging, one that reaches deeply into what had been separated out during the late twentieth century as the middle class.

Of special interest to me are the mechanisms through which social strata are reproduced. Education plays an outsized role in this process. Social class within capitalism is, to a much greater extent than commonly acknowledged, hereditary. But it is hereditary in an odd sense of the word. Maintaining one's social position requires considerable ongoing effort, not just for parents but for their children as well. Education is one of the key vehicles where jockeying for social position takes place. It is where the competitive process finds its fullest expression in terms of intergenerational transmission.

Education is also an implement through which smaller portions of the population are able to evade these same class strictures. For these limited numbers, education becomes the independent variable that accounts for their rise within the social hierarchy. For everyone else, education represents a barrier that prevents economic mobility. Educational limits often work in conjunction with other variables—such as gender, race, ethnicity, national origin, sexual orientation, and more— to keep people within their relative socioeconomic domains.

3

Capitalism has had a halting existence since its beginning. Not even the few brief prosperous decades after World War II could overcome capitalism's tendency to lurch from one difficult situation to another. But it has also occasioned a tremendous expansion of productive capacities and with it an enormous proliferation of commodities.

Machine-determined productivity has reached unimagined levels. Karl Marx marveled at the dexterity of the economic system when writing his magnum opus, *Capital*. Reporting on productivity within English silk factories between 1856 and 1862, he noted that the workforce had declined by 7 percent, even though the number of spindles handled by the employees increased by 27 percent, and the number of looms by 16 percent.[2] J. H. Clapham documented the immense increase in productive power in continental Europe for the entirety of the nineteenth century, while David Landes brought matters up-to-date for the next half-century, noting for instance that iron and steel production increased from 41.6 to 79.4 tons per worker per annum between 1912 and 1931.[3]

Clearly, both production and productivity increase simultaneously. The authors of *The State of Working America* calculate that "productivity grew 80.4 percent between 1973 and 2011," even though "median worker pay grew just 10.7 percent."[4] This simple comparison reveals the fate of the working population during the past decades. Measured over a 38-year period, a 10.7 percent increase in remuneration constitutes barely any change at all. Nothing since has altered this equation. Production far outstrips compensation, a circumstance that speaks to the essence of the economic system.

Education has become an intermediary institution between a social system that habitually sputters and declines while ever-greater amounts of consumer products are dangled in front of the system's workforce. The result: a dynamic fraught with all sorts of negative possibilities, both socially and psychologically. The theme to which this book is devoted is that of the re-creation of a working class that was thought to have all but evolved out of existence some decades ago. College students and their fate in the world of employment serve as a good point of entry into the class system. These students are drawn from across the class spectrum and then dispersed back into many of these same realms.

The issue of underemployment for college graduates—that is, employment in positions that do not require a four-year degree—has attracted attention periodically, whenever the percentage of graduates without adequate employment skyrocketed in comparison to previous conditions. The 1970s were one such moment. The 1990s were another.

Both periods, like today, were times of considerable economic turmoil and adjustment in the domestic and international arenas. The 1970s stand out because students had been central to the protest movements that spanned the globe. There were a host of civil rights, anti-war, identity-oriented, and national liberation movements; today, we witness Occupy, the Arab Spring, Black Lives Matter, and the rekindling of anti-authoritarian protests.

In each of these instances, the production of college graduates clashed with the ability of the system to absorb them. Richard Freeman, whose *The Overeducated American* describes this phenomenon in great detail, wrote: "recipients of ... degrees in most fields accepted salaries in the early 1970s at real rates of pay far below those of their predecessors—and often in jobs quite divorced from their field of study and well below their levels of aspiration."[5]

The 1960s rejection of American society due to endemic inequalities and constant war-making morphed during the following decade into an inability to integrate into the job market because of altered economic conditions. Half a century later, we are able to recognize a recurring pattern that was only dimly glimpsed at its onset: college graduates on a downward trajectory socially and economically.

There is, nonetheless, a critical difference between then and now. During the latter decades of the twentieth century, the college-educated population was not yet the object of economic restructuring. Instead, the deindustrialization of the factory-employed proletariat was predominant. Despite the economic stagnation that characterized the decade following their emergence from the university system, the great majority of college graduates during the 1960s and 1970s eventually found jobs, even as large portions of the working class were losing theirs. Factory-placed robots and the movement of production facilities to low-wage regions of the world was the leitmotif of a lost profitability that machines were expected to restore.

The computerization of skilled work is a more recent development, which has occurred simultaneously with the casualization of labor, that is, its partial transformation into part-time and intermittent employment. These developments deepened dramatically during the 1990s and coincided with a renewed intensification of the deindustrializing processes already underway since the 1970s.

Throughout these decades, the factory proletariat shrank as a proportion of an ever-expanding workforce. Since the turn of the new century, it has also declined in absolute numbers. The transition from a relative reduction to an absolute drop has not yet taken hold for the college-educated population. Current discussions regarding robotics, artificial intelligence, and big data suggest, however, that such a shift is not far distant.[6]

Class alone

The Educated Underclass begins with the separation of the population into discrete strata according to the level of education that individuals have achieved. I proceed by means of an outcomes assessment; in other words, I disregard educational intent and examine solely education's role in the segmentation of the population into identifiably different income levels (or "classes" in popular parlance). In Chapter 2, I examine some of the mechanisms through which upward and downward mobility become possible due to the overriding factors of economic growth (or stagnation) on the one hand, and the influence of family income and parental education on the other. The next chapter contains a short history of the interplay between higher education and social class, where I pay close attention to the stratification of the population into working- and middle-class segments during the heyday of capitalist development following World War II.

Chapter 4 includes an analysis of the last decades of the twentieth century. Even though life proceeded as if social class relations had been frozen in place, the thoroughgoing reorganization of the manufacturing and service sectors of the economy set the stage for an analogous reorganization of the workworld that college graduates inhabit. The final chapters concentrate on the re-formation of a working class that has also begun to think of itself in just those terms.

Throughout the book, I assume a reader who is not conversant with the relevant literatures, debates, and discussions from which I draw material. The endnotes are a guide to some of the many signature contributions. I have also made use of data and diagrams, since there are always multiple means to arrive at the same point. Each subfield is characterized by a far-reaching set of scholarly articles and popular books, a testament to the growth of the university system over the past three-quarters of a century.

Both quantitative and qualitative data are now available, for instance, to track the vastly different rates of college attendance, persistence, and graduation that depend on a person's family background and familial well-being, a theme addressed in the opening chapters.[7] Another subfield includes accounts by academics and professionals from working-class and poor backgrounds, as they navigate areas of society to which they were not privy as children.[8] Still other literatures exist for each topic tackled in the book. These subfields are often invisible except to those who exist within or immediately adjacent to them; in other words, these are academic fields which nonetheless can be quite helpful in teasing out salient points that warrant close scrutiny.

Much of the literature is policy-oriented, itself a form of utopian thinking within a society notoriously difficult to change in ways that work to the benefit of the general population. Despite the trenchant criticisms of specific aspects of society, the literature rarely embarks on a wider investigation into the factors that prevent policy suggestions from becoming reality. It is simply imagined that the political world can undo what the economy hath wrought and vested interests have maintained.

The market economy is at root wasteful of human talent and resources alike. The overproduction of commodities, to return to an earlier theme, is commonplace, notwithstanding economists' assertions to the contrary. No business habitually underestimates its market, with the sole exception, perhaps, of monopolistic enterprises that limit supplies in order to keep prices high. Even at the height of "monopoly capitalism" in the decades immediately following World War II, all other business activity was subject to fierce competitive pressure.

Nor are markets ever stable, a function of a competitive process that constantly reemerges due to the ever-present need for profits. By the 1970s, oligopolistic practices had declined dramatically, only to be rekindled under the new global regime that emerged subsequently. While the production process is fully planned by each business entity, demand continues to resemble the fruit and vegetable markets of yore.

These very same dynamics are replicated in the field of education, even though they are also skewed because of the role of government in the funding and regulation of that world. An extremely complicated situation awaits college graduates. For several decades, higher wages have been combined with an inability to find educationally appropriate employment, a situation that defies every tenet of the economics profession. What follows in this book is an examination of that edge of reality where education and economy produce results just the opposite of what in theory is claimed that they will do. Hence, the title: *The Educated Underclass*.

A note on race, gender, and geography

For the most part, I do not focus on issues of race and gender, not because these aren't important, but because my aim is to explicate the role of higher education in perpetuating social class divisions. As a rule, race and class run parallel to one another, in that adverse circumstances are exacerbated through their interaction. Almost anything that impacts whites negatively has impacted blacks even more so.

Integration of any sort—educational, occupational, or residential—indicates a drawing together of communities that were previously held distant. Whites are still less disadvantaged for sure, but the gulf that once separated people according to race and ethnicity has grown narrower over time. We have instead groups that suffer different intensities of deprivation—insufficient and banal, unfulfilling employment, inadequate social services, and an educational system that promises much more than it can deliver.

How one views race has direct implications for the understanding of class. These are two overlapping and mutually reinforcing characteristics that are best initially comprehended as separate dynamics in order to then understand their interactions together.

Nor is it prudent to rely on catchall categories. The concept of "latinx," for instance, masks huge differences within that population. The same is true for other categories, such as religion, national origin, and sexual orientation. Each requires a distinct mode of comprehension due to the manner by which it continues to function as a means to sort people into differential categories.

Gender takes us in altogether different directions. When restrictions are lifted and harassment reduced, women tend to outpace men in nearly every field of endeavor. The majority of high school, undergraduate, and graduate degrees are now awarded to women. Women always earned more high school diplomas in order to teach in the rapidly expanding public education system. They have earned greater numbers of associate degrees ever since 1978, bachelor's degrees since 1982, master's degrees since 1987, and doctoral degrees since 2006.[9]

While the deindustrialization of the late twentieth century simultaneously reduced men's wages and prompted them to leave the labor force, women found paid employment at unprecedented rates and with higher compensation than previously.[10] For 30 percent of married (heterosexual) couples, women now earn more than their husbands.[11] Education at all levels helped make this possible.

Deindustrialization was thus a positive social development for women, a circumstance largely overlooked within the gendered perspectives that characterize analyses of this phenomenon. There is much more to be said about how this double-sided adjustment to the workforce altered society in quite fundamental ways, but nonetheless deindustrialization also included an emancipatory component.

Race in combination with gender complicates matters once again. Single mothers within the African American community, for instance, have been subjected to woeful wages and a dearth of adequate services for themselves and their children in terms of health, housing, and education. More paid jobs may be available to them, but the employment world has since been restructured such that two full-time employees are now needed to adequately support a single family. Except for occasional mentions of prominent trends, however, I do not explore the interaction of class with race, ethnicity, or gender to any great degree.

International trends are also left out of consideration in the pages that follow, despite the prevalence of college students and underemployed college graduates in recent protest movements around the globe. To name only a few: Tunisia during the Arab Spring, Hong Kong to preserve a political system that is rapidly fading, and Quebec Province in Canada, where a popular and widespread student strike slowed the trend towards the privatization of higher education by means of tuition hikes. Elsewhere, students have become an export commodity because both the post-secondary educational systems and the domestic job markets are too limited to absorb them—India, Pakistan, Turkey, and China being outstanding examples.

1

Higher education and class

In the United States today, college students account for roughly 40 percent of all 18–24 year-olds.[1] Add in adult students and the figures go much higher. Nearly two-thirds of 25–34 year-olds have attended college for some amount of time.[2]

College students are now drawn from across the social spectrum in a manner unimaginable prior to the late twentieth century. Higher education includes a much wider array of individuals and social groups, not just males, but females too, and not just white students, but also students diversified by race, ethnicity, and geography. A kind of reshuffling of social class takes place in higher education that isn't found in primary and secondary schools, based as the latter are in economically and racially segregated neighborhoods.

Because they spend anywhere from a few months to eight entire years together, college students represent a loosely defined cohort, not fully separate from the rest of society, but with experiences unique only to themselves. This is as true for full-time undergraduates at Queens College in New York, as it is for graduate students at Stanford University in California, part-time certificate seekers at Alvin Community College in Texas, and returning adult students at Pinnacle Career Institutes in Missouri and Kansas.

College students are also perceived differently from every other sector of society. Great expectations surround each of them, no matter where they attend or what field of study they pursue. Aeronautical engineering is as invested in hope for the future as is court stenography.

Education and upward mobility are considered synonymous by just about everyone with whom a student comes into contact. Education defines who you are and how you are seen by others. "As a student," said one undergraduate, "I have a future. This is more important than any identity as a part-time employee." To be a college student is an identity to be embraced with pride, a testament to the special abilities and talents that the student has developed along their way.

But education can bring with it a certain kind of naivety about self and society. Policy discussions have focused on the factors that have thwarted students from achieving higher levels of education, income, success, and social harmony. Among the culprits: the defunding and partial collapse of the public school system, the continuing orientation of elite private schools towards the children of their alumni, the bloated claims that accompanied the expansion of the charter and faith-based educational systems, and the for-profit, proprietary school sector's rapaciousness. Teachers and parents have also come into their share of blame.

To examine more precisely the ways that colleges and universities sometimes replicate and sometimes rearrange traditional class patterns is one of the aims of this book.

* * *

Despite common assumptions about upward mobility, college students are also filtered back into all levels of society. The Federal Reserve Bank of New York reports that two out of every five graduates from four-year institutions work in jobs which don't require a college education. These figures cover all graduates between the ages of 22 and 27, a substantial group to find itself underemployed.[3]

Still other graduates are thrust into "precarious" work, the so-named "gig economy" that includes part-time and fixed-term employment contracts. Estimates peg this segment between 10–35 percent of the workforce nationwide, depending on whether the data is limited to primary employment or includes incomes based on part-time and multiple sources.[4] Even more depressing outcomes await college students who don't graduate or who receive a credential less than a four-year degree.

Taken as a whole, the gig economy with its underemployment and precarious work schedules now defines reality for the majority of graduates. Some find that they are unable to duplicate the lifestyle and career trajectories of their parents. For them, downward mobility has become a by-product of higher education.

In the case of information specialists working on short-term contracts, for instance, a college education can open the way to a stalled mobility. Without the degree, these high-paying but limited forms of employment would not be possible. Six months at $2,000 per week is a great salary for a 24-year-old who has no dependents and is still covered through her parents' health insurance. But what happens when the gig is over?

For others, upward mobility has been forestalled, as if they exist in a permanent holding pattern. Higher education represents a road to nowhere, a glass ceiling separating graduates from tantalizing opportunities that cannot be reached. A college graduate working as a barista at a coffee shop suffers from both underemployment and precarious work. This isn't a gig, but instead represents life itself. As one college graduate expressed it, serving coffee and sandwiches on weekends was fine when he was still a student, but once he had graduated, he needed a "real" job, one with steady pay, health benefits, paid vacations and time off—and a career trajectory that led into the future.

The fate of college students is only one element in the shift of social classes currently under way. The entire socioeconomic spectrum is experiencing a fast-paced realignment that has major ramifications for just about everyone. The expansion of the upper class is another such piece. The wealthy are more numerous, both in absolute numbers and as a percentage of the population, and more affluent. The result: a huge and ever-growing divide between them and everyone else.

How the rich got richer is well documented, with extensive coverage in scholarly journals and the popular press.[5] Speculative markets that favor stock ownership and certain types of real estate, combined with realignment of the tax system and periodic enhancements of governmental funds to save the banking system and infuse a sluggish economy, were the principal means of wealth acquisition. Added to this is the ability of the rich to increase their own salaries, perks, bonuses, and benefits in a winner-take-all situation that finds various marketplace rationalizations.

Nothing so favorable has benefited middle-income families, whose earnings have barely risen in a half-century. Certain segments have been peeled off rather dramatically, with considerable hardship on the part of everyone caught in any of the recent economic upheavals. The mortgage crisis and Great Recession of 2008 mostly affected new entrants into homeownership. For the first time, rather than paying a fixed monthly rent, homeowners sent monthly payments to banks through a process that obscured the real costs of debt. Because of foreclosures, the number of home-owning households dropped by several million over a five-year period.

Deindustrialization and the loss of full-time, benefit-bearing, and relatively well-paid employment in manufacturing has been a second major avenue of downward mobility. These jobs were replaced by lower-paid and mostly part-time work in the service sector, a by-product of the fundamental shift taking place both domestically and globally. Some tens of millions of employees have been caught in these dynamics ever since the last decades of the twentieth century in a process that is still ongoing.

For these two groups, economic difficulties reaffirmed their roots within the working class. College graduates are a third peg in this free-fall, comprising something of an upper crust within that renewed constellation. Here too, the number of underemployed graduates counts in the millions. The final chapters of this book explore this new proletariat in greater detail. First, though, we need to investigate the relationship between higher education and class.

Education as stratification

Today, the educational system is as much a sorting machine as it was once a vehicle for upward mobility. At each step of the process, people are left behind, sometimes because of their own inclinations, sometimes because finances are too thin or do not support time away from the workforce, and sometimes because educational institutions require academic proficiencies that they lack. For our purposes, the results of this sorting process are its most significant aspect. Who is shed along the way, and who succeeds?

A half-century ago, attempts to create a critical "political economy of education" fell short because of assumptions about the unitary nature of society. The authors of one of the most influential books within this genre wrote that "the school system is a monument to the capacity of the advanced corporate economy to accommodate and deflect thrusts away from its foundations."[6]

This is of course true, except that the "advanced corporate economy" results from the very same social forces that created the modern system of education. The one does not explain the other. Instead, class and education mirror the economy, each developing in piecemeal fashion as society responds to specific conditions that seem both urgent and realistic at any particular time. These are complicated dynamics if only because of the ad hoc nature of how these different facets of society evolve on their own terms and also interact with one another.

Theorizing about education and the economy developed incrementally over the past century, as has data collection regarding educational attainment and social background.[7] Theory and research have accompanied the build-out of the governmental sector. Each decade, especially from the 1930s on, witnessed major leaps forward in terms of the complexity and sophistication with which we have come to understand these relationships.

Throughout the educational process, family income plays a decisive role. But money also facilitates other essential processes that co-determine educational outcomes, rather than serving as the sole or primary factor. Academic ability, on the one side, and scholarship programs, government-sponsored grants, and student loans on the other, alter in fundamental ways the functioning and importance of family. None of these factors are fully independent of the others; after all, virtually all education beyond the secondary level requires some degree of non-governmental funding.

Of note at the outset is the overwhelming nature of this system. Only 80 percent of high school students graduate on time, with another 10–15 percent or so needing extra years to complete this stage of their education. A full 30 percent of high school students do not pursue education beyond this point.[8] By the end of adolescence, a significant sorting process has taken place, with nearly a third of the population dropping out of the educational pipeline.

Much of this outcome is predestined, based not only on factors such as family income and parental education, but also on many of the derivatives of these two factors, such as access to pre-school experiences, funding for primary and secondary schools, class size and teacher attention, household and residential stability, and more. The net effect of mandatory childhood education (until the age of 16) is to postpone the sorting of the population until the late adolescent years.

Among the students who continue their education past high school, a further sorting immediately takes place. Some high school graduates will attend two-year community colleges, others four-year baccalaureate institutions. Community college students account for a third of all college attendees, some 6.5 million out of 20 million, as of 2015.[9] Thus, at the cusp of adulthood, the population has been segmented into three primary groups: the high school educated, those who will receive limited amounts of post-secondary education (including a two-year associate's degree), and those who will receive a baccalaureate or graduate degree.

This matters because education correlates with income. The more education, the higher on average your future earnings (Table 1.1).[10]

The differences are significant. The recipient of a four-year bachelor's degree has double the annual earnings of someone who did not finish high school. The gap between a four-year degree and a high school diploma (the so-named "college premium") is also substantial, a divide that over time has only grown wider.

Table 1.1 Earnings by educational attainment

Less than high school	$25,360
High school completion	$31,830
Some college, no degree	$34,900
Associate's degree	$38,000
Bachelor's degree	$49,990
Graduate degrees	$64,070

Source: NCES, *Digest of Education Statistics: 2017*, Table 502.30.

Family income and parental education

Family income and parental education jointly help to determine how much education an individual will likely receive. Consequently, low- and high-income families inhabit two different worlds. An important study from a decade ago scrutinized 15,400 high school sophomores who attended a variety of public, private, and parochial schools.[11] At the low end were poverty- or near poverty-level families with annual incomes below $20,000. At the high end were families with incomes above $100,000. Some of these constituted the stable "middle class," others were part of the upper rungs of society.

In low-income families, nearly half of the children never made it beyond high school, and only one-fifth attended a four-year college or university, with the remainder either attending a two-year institution or a postsecondary program of even shorter duration. With wealthier families, an overwhelming 69.5 percent opted to attend a four-year institution. No other group takes as much advantage of the educational system. A full 90 percent of the high-income group enrolled in some form of postsecondary education.

Parental education is just as important as income for determining the amount of education an individual will receive. The more educated the parents, the more likely that the children will continue their education beyond high school. Many students acknowledge that during family discussions, attending college was simply assumed and not left for them to decide at some future point. Choice for adolescents, ironically, often indicates a family status lower down the income ladder.

Strong parent-child linkages lend a decided caste-like quality to the transmission of social class across generations. For parents who did not go beyond high school, slightly more than half (53.1 percent) of their children seek more education than they had by attending college. In college-educated households, the great majority of children attempt to replicate what their parents have already achieved, with college attendance rates of over 80 percent.

Naturally, these two groups of parents conceptualize education and the future differently, attitudes that are echoed by their children in terms of self-perceptions, aspirations, and expectations. Thoughts about the future are internalized long before actual choices are made. From the same high school cohort noted above, only the high-income group exhibited a strict congruence between aspirations to attend college (89.9 percent) and actual enrollment (90.7 percent). A significant gap opens between them and their lower-income classmates, of whom only one-half to two-thirds are as likely to take a college entrance exam, apply for admission, or enroll in college immediately following high school.[12]

Both groups express their social status by how they judge the future. Fewer low-income students partake in the college preparation process of exams and applications, and this underscores their lower expectations regarding future education. The further down the income hierarchy, the larger the gap between aspirations and accomplishments, as if a huge barrier had suddenly been imposed on the dreams of children.

Family income and parental education reinforce and magnify one another. When parents lack advanced education, it weighs heavily on the fate of their children. High family income alone cannot offset the negative pull exerted by the educational status of less-educated parents.

Remarkably, as seen in Figure 1.1, only 32 percent of children from the highest income level manage to graduate from college if their parents didn't graduate. This rate of

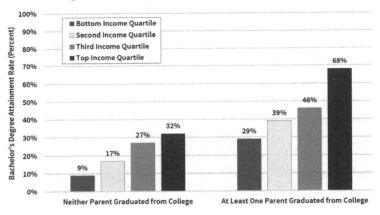

Figure 1.1   Educational attainment of parents[13]

Source: William G. Bowen, Matthew M. Chingos, and Michael S. McPherson, *Crossing the Finish Line: Completing College at America's Public Universities* (Princeton University Press, 2009), pp. 21, 272 n.1. Data from the National Education Longitudinal Study, 1988/2000. Reproduced with permission: Princeton University Press.

success is barely better than that of bottom-tiered descendants of college-educated parents. For those children, the highest income group has a success rate double that of the similarly well-off families in which parents lack college degrees (68 vs. 32 percent). In all, there is a seven-fold difference in graduation rates from the lowest to the highest, when both family income and parental education are taken into account.

This combination of factors—high family income and college-educated parents—essentially defines the upper strata in the United States. Single factors alone do not propel children at significant rates. Except for a tiny portion of the population in which inherited wealth provides substantial income and hence negates the need for advanced education, family finances are insufficient to guarantee future success.

Because neither family income nor parental education are wholly predictive in terms of educational outcomes, the transmission of class across generations follows highly individualized routes. Nonetheless, the results when taken as a whole are unsurprising. We might not know who will wind up where, but we do know that there will be a huge gulf separating those at the top from those at the bottom. At all points, education plays a critical and divisive role in the stratification of the population.

Community colleges

All segments of the educational pipeline contain powerful sorting mechanisms. High schools represent a first tier. The second is occupied by the two-year community colleges, which, as mentioned earlier, educate one-third of the collegiate population. These students receive nowhere near the same amount of attention as students at the more prestigious four-year schools, in terms of neither scholarly inquiry nor resources. We just don't know much about them, even though, in comparison, enormous efforts have gone into understanding outcomes at the four-year institutions.

In most discussions, authors simply assume that "college" refers to a four-year school, a throwback to the time when two-year institutions were still referred to as "junior colleges." Prominent scholars write that community colleges are "often the schools of last resort and those that bring college the closest to the people." The authors don't specify who "the people" are, nor is it quite accurate to state that community colleges are a "last resort."[14] For both academic and financial reasons, they are often the *only* resort for students who attend them. This difference in emphasis is important. It's not that students make limited choices, but that the options available to them are limited.[15]

The community colleges are a key element in the process that divides the population into distinct social strata. Community colleges' primary focus is occupational training. Besides the two-year associate's degrees, they also offer employment-related certificates. These are mostly prerequisites for government-regulated licensure.[16] The latter has become increasingly important over the past half-century.

More than one in four employees nationwide now holds some sort of certification or license, without which they would not have been hired. They work in a wide range of occupations, such as bookkeeping and payroll clerks, preschool aides, addiction counselors, restaurant workers, environmental technicians, medical assistants, personal trainers, plumbers, and hundreds of other employment fields.[17] While students from the four-year institutions will inhabit the middle and upper echelons of business and government, the two-year students, with their certificates and associate's degrees, will populate various parts of the service-oriented lower- and middle-income proletariat.

Some certificates are acquired easily and quickly: food handlers in New York City, for instance, earn a certificate after 15 self-paced online lessons and a fee of $24.60. College enrollment is not necessary, nor is mastery of the English language. Other programs, however, require lengthier periods of instruction and practical experience. A certificate in computer-aided design technology requires several semesters of college coursework.[18]

Nationally, similar numbers of certificates and associate's degrees are awarded, about 1 million of each annually, not just by community colleges but by for-profit institutions as well. A small percentage of certificate programs require two to four years to complete, but the majority are finished in one to two years. Most students (over 90 percent) enroll under "open admissions" policies in which a high school diploma (or equivalency) is sufficient.[19]

The gap between aspirations and accomplishments mentioned earlier in the chapter is evident at the community colleges. Nearly half the students are filtered out before they finish anything. An important and widely cited report (similar to the report on high school sophomores) documented that nearly all the entering students (86 percent) expected to earn either a certificate or a degree. Many had lofty hopes that included transfer to a four-year institution, followed by graduate school.

Six years after their initial enrollment, fewer than half had achieved that goal. Just over a third of the original group (36 percent) had earned a certificate, associate's degree, or bachelor's degree (the latter by transferring to a four-year institution). Of the remainder, 17 percent were still taking classes. The other 47

percent were no longer enrolled. The majority had settled for
less than what they intended:[20]

Table 1.2 Community college outcomes

Outcome	Intended outcome (per cent)	Actual outcome after six years (per cent)
Certificate	5%	10%
Associate's degree	10%	16%
Bachelor's degree	37%	10%
Graduate degree	34%	No data
Did not know/no credential	14%	Not applicable
Transferred/still enrolled	Not applicable	17%
No longer enrolled	Not applicable	47%

Compiled from: Thomas R. Bailey, D. Timothy Leinbach, and Davis Jenkins, "Is Student Success Labeled Institutional Failure? Student Goals And Graduation Rates In The Accountability Debate At Community Colleges," http://ccrc. tc.columbia.edu, September 2006, pp. 1 n.1, 2, 20.

The divergence between intentions and accomplishments may be ubiquitous throughout the educational pyramid, but it works differently for students who start near the bottom than for students from the top of the social scale. For the bottom group, it blocks upward mobility. For the upper group, it foretells a downward trajectory.

Institutional selectivity

Although stratification is ubiquitous throughout American society, it is also a highly nuanced system.[21] Where one is educated—the precise institution—matters greatly. Gaps in entry-level earnings emerge not only between the graduates of two-year community colleges and four-year baccalaureate institutions, but within the hierarchy of four-year institutions as well.

All colleges and universities are ranked according to their degree of competitiveness, a system that helps determine, and is also determined by, the number of applications received and the scholastic level of the applicant pool. The more competitive the school, the more prestigious it is to attend and the more selective the school can be. A school's ranking also affects the amount of private donations, private and public contracts, and government grants that it receives.

Selectivity rankings are based on applicants' college entrance exam scores, high school grades, rank-in-class, and the percent of applicants who gain admission and then enroll, with the latter referred to as the "yield." Still other ranking systems use an expanded list of criteria to determine the educational hierarchy, such as faculty publications, student amenities, and peer institution assessments, but the caliber of the applicant pool remains the heart of all such systems.

"Noncompetitive" schools require only a high school diploma (or equivalency) for admission. These are known as "open admissions" institutions, a category which not only includes most two-year community colleges, but also many four-year institutions. Half of all collegiate institutions are included in this category, including one-quarter of all four-year schools.[22] The open admissions policies of the two-year colleges are part of what makes it possible for the four-year public colleges and universities to maintain higher standards. Virtually anyone who wants to attend college can find an institution that will accept them.

An example of a four-year non-competitive school is Presentation College in South Dakota, where "prospective students must graduate from high school or hold a GED, and a GPA of 2.0 [C] is recommended." It offers certificate programs, and associate's and bachelor's degrees to 630 full- and part-time students.[23]

At a "less competitive" school, minimal standards apply. Acceptance rates are typically above 85 percent, and applicants with high school averages below a "C" level and ranking only in the top 65 percent of their class are admitted customarily. Bloomfield College in New Jersey, for instance, reports that "15% of the current freshmen were in the top fifth of their class; 41% were in the top two fifths."[24] Left unsaid are the other 44 percent who ranked at the 40th percentile or below in high school.

In the "most and highly competitive" institutions, on the other hand, applicants need exemplary records in terms of high school rankings, grades, and scores on standardized tests, as well as outstanding letters of recommendation, a history of volunteer and athletic participation, and more. Elite institutions ordinarily admit less than one-third of the applicants. Even applicants with perfect scores on the standardized admissions exams are rejected, so intense is the competition. At Macalester College in Minnesota, only 41 percent of applicants were accepted. A full 88 percent were in the top fifth of their high school class. At Yale University in Connecticut, only 7 percent of applicants were accepted. Over 80 percent of the applicants scored between 700 and 800, the maximum range, on each of the three sections of the Scholastic Aptitude Test (Critical Reading, Math, Writing).[25]

All this is noteworthy because institutional selectivity correlates with future earnings. One study reported average mid-career salaries of $104,597 for graduates of "elite private institutions," $87,274 for "state flagship institutions," and $67,063 for "other state institutions."[26] Entry-level earnings confirm the intense stratification determined by the selectivity of the institution attended:[27]

Table 1.3 Entry-level earnings of graduates, by institutional selectivity

Community colleges	$33,177
Less and non-competitive colleges	$37,081
Competitive colleges	$39,880
Very competitive colleges	$41,779
Most and highly competitive colleges	$53,817

Source: Anthony P. Carnevale and Jeff Strohl, "How Increasing College Access Is Increasing Inequality, and What to Do about It," Georgetown University Center on Education and the Workforce, in *Rewarding Strivers: Helping Low-Income Students Succeed in College*, Richard D. Kahlenberg, ed. (Century Foundation Press, 2010), p. 145.

Students from top-tier institutions started their careers earning nearly $17,000 more than students educated at "less and non-competitive" colleges.

It is not just the *amount* of education someone receives that is important, but also *where* they receive that education: similar educations at dissimilar institutions produce dissimilar results. Status outranks content, even though institutional rankings need not correlate with the quality of the education offered. This finely grained system of differentiations contributes to the layering of the population into discreet strata.

Social background

Academic institutions tend to be fairly homogeneous in terms of the academic abilities of their students. This means that the relative selectivity of the institution correlates with the socioeconomic profile of its student body. At the "less and non-competitive" institutions, depicted in Figure 1.2, students are

recruited from the population at large in roughly equal proportions. Each quartile of the population is represented by
one-quarter of the students.

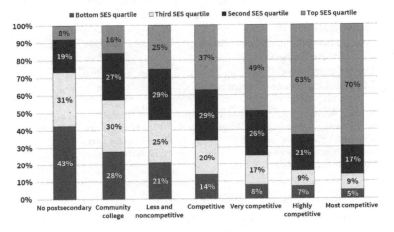

Figure 1.2   Student socioeconomic background and institutional
selectivity, 2006

Source: Anthony P. Carnevale and Jeff Strohl, "How Increasing College Access
Is Increasing Inequality, and What to Do about It," in *Rewarding Strivers*,
pp. 118–120, 137. Reproduced with permission: Georgetown University Center
on Education and the Workforce and Century Foundation Press.

Thus, the most egalitarian of educational institutions are
the ones that have minimal entrance requirements beyond the
attainment of a high school degree. These are the only four-year
institutions for which this is true. However, they handle less
than 10 percent of the entire collegiate population. All other
collegiate institutions are considerably more biased in terms of
the socioeconomic backgrounds of their students.[28]

The more selective and exclusive the institution, the wealthier,
on average, the students' background. "Competitive" institutions accept students from the upper socioeconomic quartile

at more than twice the rate of students from the lower quartile (37 vs. 14 percent). At the upper end, the "most competitive" institutions are inhabited overwhelmingly (70 percent) by students whose families are in the top quartile socioeconomically. A columnist in the *New York Times* concludes that "higher education, once seen as the nation's great leveler, has become a guardian of class division and privilege in America."[29] All social classes are represented at all educational institutions, but the most selective and privileged institutions are overwhelmingly attended by members of the upper classes.

Education is not so much a vehicle for upward mobility as it is a means to maintain a family's social position from generation to generation. One student stated that what she wanted in life was "nothing less than what I have already." As a rule too, the more selective the institution, the higher the tuition. It is on this level that family income becomes a direct determinant of educational outcomes. While publicly funded schools have lifted the economic fortunes of broad swaths of the population, reaching the highest rungs depends heavily on the resources of the elite. Financial wherewithal becomes self-perpetuating. Lower-income students are funneled out simply because they cannot afford to attend the expensive institutions.[30]

Quite a lot is known about the familial processes that make institutional selectivity possible. A wide array of personal services exist to foster children's educational success. Upper-tier families live, almost without exception, in income-segregated neighborhoods. They either send their children to private schools or live in areas where public education did not collapse decades ago. They also hire private tutors, ensure that their children take advanced placement exams, and generally engage in enrichment activities that are valued by collegiate institutions. Thomas J. Espenshade and Alexandria Walton Radford, authors of *No Longer Separate, Not Yet Equal*, a comprehensive study of admissions practices at elite schools, summarize these practices:

> High SES [socioeconomic status] parents are more likely to pay for test preparation courses, take trips to visit colleges the summer before their children's senior year, know how and when to interact with school guidance counselors about the college choice process, and hire an independent counselor to assist in selecting schools and preparing applications. During the choice phase, high SES parents are more likely to encourage early applications (with the knowledge that acceptance rates are higher then than during the regular application period), remind their children of tasks they need to complete and help them make and keep a schedule, assist with personal essays, review an application before it is submitted, pay for application to multiple colleges, and bear the responsibility of paying for college.[31]

Other studies have documented the childrearing practices specific to upper-income families. One of the best-known examples demonstrates how children from college-educated households are exposed to a wider range of vocabulary and syntax in the course of everyday conversation. Growing up in an educated household confers distinct advantages regarding language and cognitive development.[32]

Advantages are expensive to maintain, however, because they rest so thoroughly on a mode of existence that requires heavy inputs of financial resources. The focus on individual achievement presupposes a wide range of services and personnel to guide students in quite precise ways. The steady schedule of artistic, sports, and other extracurricular activities entails fees, memberships, and equipment as well as the time to ferry children to and from them. One estimate put a cost of $8,872 per year for the "enrichment expenditures" of children from the top quintile and $1,315 for those from the bottom.[33]

Because the system of educational advantage is so comprehensive in scope, programs that target single variables or a limited set of constituent processes—such as mathematics tutoring, subsidized college applications, self-confidence, or the easy transferability of credits—often have a limited overall impact. Educational advantage is the product of how the entire social system is structured. Access does not constitute equality.

Interestingly, it is considerably more expensive to maintain privilege than to overcome disadvantage. A long list of successful mass-based educational programs has demonstrated just this: the G.I. Bill of the late 1940s, the expansion of the university system during the 1950s and 60s, the Head Start program beginning in the mid-1960s, various collegiate equal opportunity programs funded by individual states, and the many grant programs sponsored on both federal and state levels that have increased access for underrepresented groups racially, ethnically, and socioeconomically.

Minimum thresholds, rather than individual excellence, were used as the basis to award benefits, with indicators such as gross income, veteran status, and financial need serving this purpose. It is clear that relying on the resources and know-how of individual family units has everything to do with class and little to do with equity.

Upper higher education

Membership in the elite was once thought to result from a process of "social darwinism." Inherited traits, so it went, were perfected within society's competitive struggle of all-against-all, with the result that the very best rose to the top of society's pecking order. This combination of heredity and worldly accomplishment was expressed by means of personal wealth, family connections, gender, race, ethnicity, and religion.

Today's elites, on the other hand, think more in terms of a meritocracy, in which their own intelligence and drive have propelled them to the top. Advanced education serves as their proof that this is true. In their opinion, great riches are something they deserve. They have earned what they reap. Inborn traits represent a bygone era.

There is broad acceptance among the elite that education represents a means of social uplift. If only everyone could be like them. Since access to higher education is available to all, individual initiative becomes the critical variable that divides the successful from everyone else. The idea that the educational system is a means to protect already-existent privileges is rarely broached. Ultimately, the ideology of access confirms rather than undermines the social darwinian aspects of class-based society.

At each tier of the educational process, additional winnowing takes place. Who goes to college, how much postsecondary education they receive, the caliber of the institution they attend, and who graduates, demonstrate the advantages of coming from a privileged background. The more select the institution—and wealthier the student body—the higher the graduation rate.[34] The "most competitive" four-year institutions show graduation rates of 88 percent; the noncompetitive rate hovers around 35 percent.[35]

Within individual institutions, family background further divides the student body. Graduation rates vary according to the students' socioeconomic background, even when all other variables, such as scores on college admissions tests and advanced placement exams, are held constant. At top-tier institutions, the children from families in the bottom socioeconomic quartile have a graduation rate of 76 percent, while students from the top quartile have a rate of 90 percent. The students are receiving a similar overall education, yet family background continues to be a factor.[36]

Just as telling are the differences that emerge within each socioeconomic stratum. Students from the high-income group graduate at a 90 percent rate from top-tier institutions but only at a 58 percent rate from the bottom tier, a significant 32-point difference. Students from the bottom socioeconomic group similarly perform much more poorly at lower-tiered institutions. If the rate of success is 76 percent at top-tier institutions, it plummets to 40 percent at the low-tiered ones.

Poorer students are negatively affected by both their backgrounds and the types of institutions they attend, whereas their wealthier peers benefit from these same factors. Even though institutional reputations are based on academic quality and scholastic standards, at the most elite schools other factors are equally important. In the words of one analyst, "the average effect of education at all levels is to reinforce rather than compensate for the differences associated with family background."[37] If higher education tilts towards the rich, it also sorts people into the very social groups that they were predetermined to inhabit.

The majority of four-year institutions practice some form of exclusivity. The "most and highly competitive colleges" handle one-fifth of everyone who attends a baccalaureate institution, a proportion roughly in sync with the size of the upper-income stratum in the United States. The breakdown is:

Table 1.4   Distribution of students, by institutional selectivity

Most competitive colleges	7.9%
Highly competitive colleges	12.9%
Very competitive colleges	24.9%
Competitive colleges	41.5%
Less competitive colleges	8.8%
Non-competitive colleges	4.0%

Source: Frederick M. Hess, Mark Schneider, Kevin Carey, and Andrew P. Kelly, "Diplomas and Dropouts: Which Colleges Actually Graduate Their Students (and Which Don't)," www.aei.org, June 2009, p. 7.

The authors of *No Longer Separate, Not Yet Equal* are unnecessarily tentative in their conclusions when they write:

Attending a more selective institution is associated with a higher probability of graduating, and graduates from elite colleges are more likely to enter leading graduate and professional schools. Second, there is a positive economic return to a college education, and the increase in this financial payoff has been a prime source of rising income inequality since the 1980s. Students who attend colleges with higher student-average SAT [Scholastic Aptitude Test] scores, higher tuition, or a variety of other measures of college "quality" tend to have even higher labor market earnings later in life.[38]

Some studies go so far as to calculate the precise monetary relationship between SAT scores and gains in income.[39] Within the elite schools, social darwinian self-replication occurs by means of family income and parental education. Academic achievement is a by-product of these same pre-conditions.[40] Despite the self-flattery that accompanies the doctrine of meritocracy as a justification for social stratification, embedded processes underlie social and economic relations as presently constructed.[41]

Educational shifts

The educational system functions as an inverted funnel through which the class system reproduces itself quite literally. The more selective the institution, the more elite its constituency. Nonetheless, it is a funnel that has grown broader over time. More people pass through each level than ever before, a process that has been ongoing for many decades.

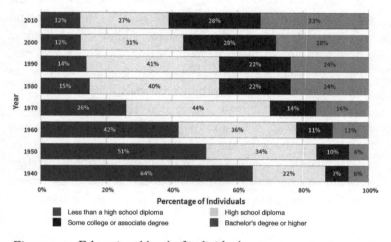

Figure 1.3   Educational level of individuals age 25–34, 1940–2010[42]

Source: Sandy Baum, Jennifer Ma, and Kathleen Payea, "Education Pays 2013: The Benefits of Higher Education for Individuals and Society," https://trends. collegeboard.org, p. 41. Data derived from U.S. Census Bureau, 2012, Table A-1. Reproduced with permission: The College Board.

The majority of 25–34 year-olds (Figure 1.3) in the United States now has some level of collegiate experience. Viewed

37

conversely, however, a similar majority has not completed enough education to earn a two-year associate's degree.[43] The population remains as deeply stratified by education as ever, though stratified in new ways. At the top of the pecking order are the 30+ percent who have graduated from a four-year institution.

Two separate yet interlinked processes are at work: the overall elevation of educational credentials throughout the population and also its re-stratification on a higher level. That these take place simultaneously is part of what makes the lived reality of class so confusing. Each generation experiences a class system that has been remade during their lifetimes, such that the reckoning points of their parents are already out-of-date and only partially usable. During the 1940s, a high school diploma represented an advanced degree. During the 1960s and '70s, a bachelor's degree took its place. Today, graduate degrees are gradually crowding out all other credentials.

To have a baccalaureate degree is to be part of a minority. But it is not as small a minority as it once was, a circumstance that leads us back to the underemployed college graduates. They join other casualties caught in the dysfunctional interface between and within the worlds of education and employment. Together, these groups comprise an educated underclass.

2

The overproduction of intelligence

The majority of students—and their parents—once believed that a college degree conferred success. The truth, as we have seen, is vastly more complicated. Each piece of the original equation regarding education and upward mobility has been whittled away, and what remains is as much illusion as it is reality.

No one, for instance, anticipated that a degree in political science would lead to years spent working as a crew chief for a window-washing and gutter-cleaning company, or that a degree from one of the most prestigious institutions nationwide could mean marginal employment in the creative arts and living at home with Mom at the age of 28. Situations like these are no longer the exception. Hope has replaced belief, and bitterness has crept in where once there was certainty. Graduates dream of a "lucky break," rather than striding forth with confidence about themselves and the future.

Researchers from the Federal Reserve Bank have charted in detail the dire employment situation for recipients of 4-year college degrees. While "individuals just beginning their careers often need time to transition into the labor market," they report, something other than a short-term changeover is occurring. Their focus is "the percentage who are unemployed or 'underemployed'—working in a job that typically does not require a bachelor's degree." The Federal Reserve authors also emphasize that "such difficulties are not a new phenomenon," but in fact have existed for several decades already.

As if the situation is not bad enough, "the quality of jobs held by the underemployed has declined." The result: "today's recent graduates increasingly accepting low-wage jobs or working part-time."[1] This collection of depressing news— underemployment, low wages, and part-time employment—is now a permanent feature of the economic landscape.

Underemployment for all college graduates of four-year institutions, whether they just graduated at the age of 22 or are on the cusp of retirement at 65, has hovered in the 30–35 percent range since the early 1990s. The 2001 recession, called the "dot.com bust" because of its impact on newly established firms within the computer industry, and the more recent Great Recession of 2008, brought all this into the open.

Economic crises tend to precipitate large-scale changes. Crises also draw attention to pertinent trends, and they clarify any doubts as to what is merely episodic and what is here to stay as the new face of the future. Underemployment for college graduates is one such phenomenon. One estimate nearly a decade ago put the total number at 17 million underemployed baccalaureate recipients.[2]

Recent college graduates are especially vulnerable. These are baccalaureate holders within the first five years of their working careers (between the ages of 22 and 27). As of September 2018, 41.5 percent had been underemployed during the previous year. Add race as a factor and the level of underemployment jumps still higher, with over half of all recently graduated black bacca-laureates underemployed.[3] One student explained that "looking for a job in this last year after graduation has been one of the most difficult and disheartening experiences of my life."

Educated and underemployed

Until a few years ago, underemployment among college graduates received little attention. A lack of good data was one reason. Without a national database, researchers relied on highly complex sampling techniques and statistical methods to arrive at estimates of the problem. Educational institutions also preferred not knowing, not necessarily because of sinister motivations, but because there was little they could do about the situation.

Colleges and universities may prepare students for the job market, but it is the job market that ultimately determines the students' destinies. A few academic units, like law schools, track precisely the fate of their graduates, but these tend to be small specialized programs, often post-baccalaureate, in which alumni remain in contact and programs retain databases that can be tapped for information. Other educational institutions do not have access to this level of information, nor do they devote many resources to such tasks. Information about successful graduates, as in medical school admissions or prestigious fellowships, is one thing; data on underemployed graduates is another.

For a brief period of time since 2015, the situation regarding information changed considerably. Until the data was withdrawn from public scrutiny, we had access to information that was unimaginable in previous decades. But also, the more we learned, the gloomier the situation revealed itself to be. The government had begun tracking information about each higher education institution on "the share of former students earning more than $25,000, or about the average earnings of a high school graduate aged 25–34, six years after they first enroll."[4] In other words, underemployment—as measured by income— was a specific focus (whereas the researchers from the Federal

41

Reserve measure college graduates in jobs for which a college education is not a requirement).

Success was defined as earning more than your high school-educated peers. The data also allowed us to see how the problem of underemployment affects institutions disproportionately. An upper-tier establishment like Princeton University reported a six-year graduation rate of 97 percent and average salaries of $80,500 ten years post-enrollment. The most relevant data from our perspective concerned underemployment. Until it was removed from the website, the data showed that 17 percent of the students who received federal financial aid earned no more than the average high school graduate.

At nearby Kean University, a state-sponsored institution, the respective figures were a 49 percent graduation rate and $46,000 salary ten years post-enrollment. Only two-thirds of its graduates earned more than the average high school graduate. In the same general commuting region, Raritan Valley Community College had a three-year graduation rate of 22 percent. Salaries ten years after enrollment averaged $35,800 per year. Only 59 percent of its graduates earned more than their high school-educated colleagues.

When nationwide over 40 percent of recent college graduates and one-third of all graduates remain underemployed, optimism about the future becomes increasingly difficult.[5] Only a quarter of the original underemployed group eventually finds work commensurate with their education. As the graduates age, their ability to locate an appropriate position improves, but only somewhat. The rest are either permanently underemployed or else float between the two categories, exchanging their status with other graduates who are similarly experiencing the same tumultuous changes in status and salary.

The circumstances surrounding alternative employment have also deteriorated. Some jobs that do not require a college degree nonetheless pay decently. "Good non-college jobs" are defined by the Federal Reserve authors as those with a "full-time average annual wage of roughly $45,000 or more." Included are professions such as electrician, dental hygienist, and mechanic. These types of jobs have declined since the turn of the new century, from a peak of 49.5 percent held by "recent [underemployed] college graduates" in April 2001 to 34.4 percent in September 2018. For all underemployed college graduates (aged 22–65), just over half (55.6 percent) had good non-college jobs in January 2001. As of September 2018, this had declined to 43.8 percent. Good jobs have disappeared.

The percent of graduates with "low-waged jobs," those that "tend to pay around $25,000 or less," hasn't changed as dramatically. Low-waged jobs encompass occupations such as bartending, food service, and cashiering. These are jobs that characterize the working poor, jobs with salaries so low that independent living isn't possible. In January 1990, 8.6 percent of recent college graduates fell into this category. This number has increased since, reaching 13.3 percent in September 2018. The corresponding figures for all college graduates inched up from 6.1 percent in 1990 to 7.4 percent.[6]

Between these two poles of "good non-college jobs" and "low-waged jobs" lies an occupational purgatory where the other one-third of underemployed college graduates reside. For them, too, success as measured by income and occupation is elusive.

Most people have rather out-of-date images of social mobility, in which people's lives improve gradually but steadily over long periods of time due to a combination of decent salaries and stable employment. This image no longer fits reality. Not an escalator leading upward, but an elevator shaft opening into an abyss, is the appropriate metaphor. Downward mobility tends to be cataclysmic when it occurs. For women and children, this has long been the case. The critical issues for them have been divorce (or separation) and illness, both of which have calamitous effects on the remaining families. Job loss is a third precipitous factor. The inability to find educationally appropriate work is still another. For college graduates, both men and women are vulnerable.

Underemployed college graduates have, for the most part, been spared the worst of this fate, but only because they occupy jobs that previously were held by people with less education. This is what accounts for the half now in "good non-college jobs" and the third that have so far avoided the "low-waged jobs." Not quite as comfortable were the 18 percent of telemarketers, 23.5 percent of "amusement and recreation attendants," 16.5 percent of bartenders, and 14.3 percent of waiters and waitresses who are college graduates and at one point were counted as part of the working poor.[7]

College graduates are part of a process that ricochets down the employment chain. Because they cannot find work commensurate with their educations, they compete for jobs that otherwise would be filled by people with other sets of credentials. How ironic that education becomes a factor that sharpens the competition over jobs, income, and material well-being.

* * *

Unemployment, rather than underemployment, has traditionally served as a barometer of collegiate success. Unemployment rates for college graduates have also remained low historically, at no point surpassing the 5.0 percent mark during the last quarter-century. This is quite favorable in comparison to other groups of employees. Among recent college graduates (22–27 year-olds), the average unemployment rate for the twelve months preceding September 2018 was 3.6 percent. The corresponding rate for their non-college educated peers was 7.2 percent.[8] Yet, unemployment only tells part of the story and masks the much broader issue of underemployment.

Underemployment is ubiquitous throughout the collegiate world. No field of study is immune. Pre-professional fields such as business management, communications, and criminal justice are often preferred by students and parents who assume that of all the educational options available to undergraduates these will provide the best conduit into full-time employment. Unfortunately, these areas also have some of the worst track records. The situation for recent college graduates of four-year institutions is as follows:[9]

Table 2.1 Pre-professional majors (non-technical)

Discipline	Unemployed	Underemployed	Total
Business management	4.2%	59.6%	63.8%
Communications	3.9%	54.8%	58.7%
Criminal justice	4.6%	75.5%	80.1%
Marketing	3.0%	53.3%	56.3%
Public policy and law	3.9%	66.2%	70.1%

A 2017 criminal justice graduate commented, "if I had known how bad job prospects were, I might have chosen another field." The logic is correct, but the options are not so clear. How do you choose between fields when the best outcome is one of relative disadvantage? The question becomes: which field leaves you less worse off than another?

That disciplines within the humanities and social sciences also fare badly won't surprise many people, as we have become accustomed to the general disparagement of these areas despite their continued, even if diminishing, popularity among students and employers:

Table 2.2   Liberal arts majors

Discipline	Unemployed	Underemployed	Total
Art history	3.2%	55.4%	58.6%
Ethnic studies	4.8%	50.5%	55.3%
History	5.5%	51.2%	56.7%
Political science	5.0%	50.6%	55.6%
Psychology	4.9%	49.7%	54.6%
Sociology	4.8%	52.1%	56.9%

Technologically oriented fields such as engineering, mathematics, and computers, on the other hand, tend to be at the high end of employability and compensation. Here too, nonetheless, the Federal Reserve authors found a situation of extensive collegiate-level underemployment:

Table 2.3   Science, technology, engineering, and mathematics (STEM) majors

Discipline	Unemployed	Underemployed	Total
Accounting	2.8%	25.2%	28.0%
Aerospace engineering	3.4%	24.4%	27.8%
Biochemistry	3.7%	34.4%	38.1%
Biology	5.0%	44.2%	49.2%
Business analytics	3.2%	38.4%	41.6%
Chemical engineering	3.8%	19.1%	22.9%
Computer engineering	2.8%	20.3%	23.1%
Computer science	4.4%	26.0%	30.4%
Economics	4.5%	37.4%	41.9%
Finance	3.7%	38.4%	42.1%
Mathematics	5.6%	32.0%	37.6%

Even in fields that prepare undergraduates for immediate licensure, like nursing and education, underemployment remains high:

Table 2.4 Pre-professional majors, with licensure

Discipline	Unemployed	Underemployed	Total
Nursing	2.3%	11.1%	13.4%
Early childhood education	2.3%	16.1%	18.4%
Elementary education	2.0%	16.3%	18.3%
Secondary education	2.7%	24.7%	27.4%
Special education	1.3%	17.7%	19.0%

Source: Federal Reserve Bank, *The Labor Market for Recent College Graduates: Outcomes by Major.*

Underemployment is both a pervasive feature and also a permanent fixture of post-collegiate life, irrespective of what a student studies. Some areas are affected to a greater extent than others, but no college student can assume that they are exempt from these dynamics.

But whereas it was once thought that a college education separated the population into distinct groups, boundaries have shifted. The favored areas, if we can even speak in such terms, have highly specific characteristics. In terms of employment, the most promising fields are those that lead directly to a professional license.

Not quite as favorable but still a cut above the liberal arts or pre-professional fields are those that involve quantitative skills. These are best understood as a derivative of the re-monopolization of economic activity, not just regionally and nationally as was the case a half-century ago, but now on a global scale, in which "big data," artificial intelligence, and robotics are the latest forms of mechanization.

Companies that master these competitive processes have the best chance of profiting and surviving, and for this, an elite core of highly educated and mathematically oriented employees is needed. Everything is now done in massive proportions—production, shipping and transportation, and advertising, all with a veneer of personalization conveyed through the multiple avenues of technological communication. This is where parts of the new "gig" economy are housed.

For the rest of the college-educated underemployed, the service sector is the primary alternative. This complicates the picture still further. Areas with similarly low rates of un- and underemployment are nonetheless divided by salary. In a field like nursing, where licensure is based on the combination of scientific knowledge and technical skills, salaries are high. This is not true for other areas of immediate, post-baccalaureate licensure, like early childhood and elementary education, in which a much lower salary scale prevails.

Student loans and student debt

Student debt was once viewed as a facilitator of future success, as a means to make life happen sooner.[10] It has instead become a barrier to upward mobility, a cautionary factor in an uncertain and negative job market. Debt impels people to lower their standard of living. For college graduates, it compounds the difficulties associated with underemployment. Debt payments are onerous, and they last a long time; according to a government website, a "repayment period may range from 10 years to 30 years, depending on loan amount, loan type, and repayment plan."[11] Student debt can encumber and leaden a significant portion of one's life.

Some students postpone graduate school because of it. One student explained that in hindsight she might have worked and saved first, then attended school, rather than have debt inhibit her from applying to a graduate program now that she was underemployed. Another student questioned the need for a college education when debt was the only certainty.

College is expensive. For families in the lowest fifth (quintile) of national income, tuition and fees at a two-year public institution at in-state rates typically costs 18 percent of their annual earnings. Make that a four-year (public) institution, and tuition and fees come to 43 percent of family income. If room, board, books, and other expenses are averaged in, the yearly cost for a four-year education jumps to 155 percent of average annual income for this same family unit. Without government grants, scholarships, and student loans, a typical family in this bracket would need to devote all resources for six straight years in order to pay for four years of education.

Families in the middle quintile of income don't feel these pressures as acutely. For the typical two-year public institution at in-state rates, only 5 percent of annual income is needed. This rises to 12 percent at public four-year institutions. All inclusive of costs (room, board, etc.) and 35 percent of a family's annual income is needed, still expensive but nonetheless a huge difference from the sacrifices required by families at the bottom of the income hierarchy.[12]

In absolute terms, though, the rich pay more for college, even if their cost is a smaller percent of overall income. This is because federal and state grants, as well as other forms of financial aid such as work-study, tend to favor lower-income families. According to one study, families with an income less than $30K paid on average $9,313, compared to families whose income exceeded $110K, who paid $16,614. This was at a public institution with a sticker price of $18,304.[13]

Over half of all college students use loans as a means to finance their education. For some, loans make college a feasible option. One student mentioned that loans substituted for the lack of parental wherewithal to pay for the many auxiliary costs that accompany tuition, like fees, books, and transportation. She had chosen to live at home and commute to school for the first two years to save her father from additional sacrifice.

For others, loans determine the caliber of the institution they attend. They also influence whether a residential experience in a far-off place is possible; how distant an institution is from home is also defined by social class. Not everyone embarks on multi-day road trips between their junior and senior years of high school in order to tour possible residential colleges.

For several decades already, loans have been a more important source of student funding than all state, federal, institutional, and private grant programs combined.[14] When data on older students are included, it turns out that "almost 40 percent of adults under the age of 40 had some outstanding student loan debt."[15]

It is also the case that the largest debtors—those who accumulated loans in the tens of thousands of dollars—have the lowest default rates. Graduate school students, including those at post-baccalaureate professional schools (medical, law, business, etc.), average some $40,000 of debt, yet they are also highly employable and generally earn good salaries. Chances are that they either came from or will wind up in the top quintile of family income. The higher the family income, the more selective the school that you attend, the more likely you are to attend graduate school, the more debt that you accrue, and the less that you need to be concerned about repayment schedules. Undergraduates at public four-year schools accrue considerable debt, on average some $30,000 (per debtor), but they too are not the most vulnerable population.[16]

The reality of the "student loan crisis" lies elsewhere, because—counterintuitively—the amount of debt is not the critical factor. Neither graduate students nor graduates of four-year institutions constitute the most vulnerable groups, at least in terms of loan defaults and late payments. Instead, "the highest rates of financial hardship are seen among households with relatively little outstanding student loan debt."[17]

Debtors with less than $5,000 in loans face the greatest difficulties, especially if you have attended two-year, for-profit, or non-selective schools, sectors that specialize in or target low-income students. Individuals who attended college but never finished are especially vulnerable. To default on a loan means to forego future eligibility for financial aid programs. This precludes a return to school in order to finish a degree or attend at the next level. Late payments alone wreak havoc on your access to credit. They also make future debt more expensive, thus creating a vulnerability to predatory lending practices.

There is a sad irony to student loans. The individuals from the bottom rungs of the income and education hierarchy, those who attend institutions which in the best of circumstances will leave them with marginal salaries, are then held back further by the debt payments which helped make their mobility possible in the first place. It's not the amount of debt that leads to further difficulties, but the socioeconomic background of the debtors that leaves them mired in place.

We have now come full circle, with underemployment and student loan debt as two mechanisms that are generating today's educated underclass.

Social mobility

Because researchers have followed income and wealth inequality for so many decades, we know a great deal about social mobility within capitalism.[18] This is important because it helps us understand the fate of underemployed college graduates. What happens to them is largely dependent on where they began. Starting near the top or the bottom of the income-education continuum heightens your chances of remaining within those very same realms.

With intergenerational mobility, which records changes in social position between parents and children, roughly 40 percent of the lower and upper quintiles of population experience no change from one generation to the next. This is the seemingly hereditary aspect of social class that refashions the class system into a system of castes.[19] Social class replicates itself quite literally.

A college education changes this dynamic considerably. In the first chapter, we tracked the influence of parents' education on their children's educational fortunes. In Figures 2.1a–b, we track the fate of the children independently of parental educational level (even though we know that parental education is a major determinate of socioeconomic status). Almost half (45 percent) of adults remain in the lowest quintile of income when they are: 1) raised within that income bracket, and 2) do not earn a bachelor's degree. With a bachelor's degree, only 16 percent remain in the bottom-income quintile. When viewed from the top quintile, 54 percent of those who earned a bachelor's degree remain within that upper quintile, whereas only 23 percent do the same without the degree.

These differences at the top and at the bottom attest to the importance of education as a social variable.[20]

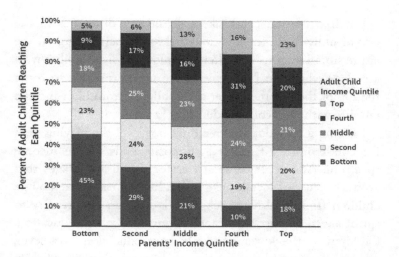

Figure 2. 1a Intergenerational income mobility—*without* a college degree

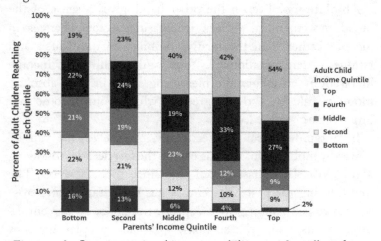

Figure 2. 1b Intergenerational income mobility—*with* a college degree

Source: Ron Haskins, "Education and Economic Mobility," in *Getting Ahead or Losing Ground: Economic Mobility in America* by Julia B. Isaacs, Isabel V. Sawhill, and Ron Haskins, p. 95, Figure 6 "Chances of Getting Ahead for Children with and without a College Degree, from Families of Varying Income." Reproduced with permission: The PEW Charitable Trusts.

But if education can make a significant difference in the fate of individuals, there is nonetheless a cruel paradox in the entire situation, since "children from low-income families with a college education [19 percent] are no more likely to reach the top of the income ladder than children from high-income families without a college education [23 percent]."[21]

Earning a bachelor's degree does not level the playing field for children from families at opposite ends of the income spectrum. At best, it compensates for the disadvantages that accrue because of social background. In the meantime, though, children from wealthier backgrounds have an opportunity to sprint ahead because they can also pursue a college education. Children at the lower end only have education as a lever, whereas their wealthier counterparts have education and family finances to help boost their way through life.

Absolute mobility, on the other hand, gives a sense of the broad movement of society. It measures actual changes in income, rather than the relative mobility of individuals and families intergenerationally. Your rank within the income hierarchy is no longer the measuring stick; instead, absolute mobility calculates the degree to which your income has improved or declined.

In a rapidly expanding economy, most everyone can be upwardly mobile. This was the case in the few decades following World War II. It hasn't been true since then, however. The trend during the past half-century has been stagnation across the entire population grid, except for the upper 20 percent. In other words, while the economy grew and people's incomes increased (absolute upward mobility), some people's incomes increased much more than others.[22] Between the late 1960s and the early years of this century, every quintile of population experienced income growth. Median income, as seen in Figure

2.2, grew from \$55,600 to \$71,900, about a 30 percent increase for the population as a whole (all figures converted into 2006 dollars). The rates of growth for each sector, however, varied wildly, from a low of 18 percent for the bottom quintile to a high of 52 percent for the top.

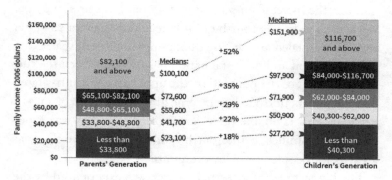

Figure 2.2 Absolute mobility—intergenerational[23]

Source: Julia B. Isaacs, "Economic Mobility of Families Across Generations," in *Getting Ahead or Losing Ground*, p. 16, Figure 1: "Change in Income Distribution from Parents' Generation to Children's Generation." Reproduced with permission: The PEW Charitable Trusts.

Quintile boundaries have also changed. For the parents to have been in the top fifth, for example, required a minimum family income of \$82,100 during the late 1960s. For their children, \$116,700 was the new cut-off at the turn of the century.

Even though each quintile experienced growth, not all families shared in it equally. For the bottom quintile, 18 percent growth meant a difference in median income of only \$4,100 (\$23,100 vs. \$27,200). Given the 30-year difference between generations, this amounts to a paltry increase of less than \$150 dollars per year. Assuming a 40-hour workweek and 50-week year, people in the lower fifth received a yearly pay raise equivalent to $.07 per hour. Accordingly, an 18 percent increase masks stagnating wages. They barely changed.

The second quintile has not fared much better. A gain of 22 percent in income translates into a yearly increase of $.15 per hour during the entire three-decade timeframe. For the third quintile, the increase amounted to $.27 per hour or $10.87 per week, each year. The fourth quintile received an extra $843 per year. This equaled an increase of $.42 per hour each year.

If stagnation and near-stagnation has therefore been the rule for 80 percent of the population, the upper 20 percent has fared considerably better. Median income grew by $51,800 or $1,728 per year. This is double the amount of growth that was experienced by families in the fourth quintile and twelve times as great as for people in the lowest quintile.[24]

The highest rate of growth, however, was experienced by the top 1 percent, who saw their incomes jump 176 percent between 1979 and 2004, more than quadruple what their colleagues in the upper quintile accrued.

Today's college graduates face a world in which the vast majority of the population has experienced only paltry income growth for the last half-century. A college education has become as much a hedge against stagnation as it is a step towards upward mobility.

The elusiveness of class

Social stratification continues to puzzle even the best of analysts. Reality has proven to be far too complex to capture in either words or images. What is it about capitalism that makes social relations so elusive? This is the puzzle that concerns us here.[25]

The most concrete understandings of class are, oddly enough, theoretical. Karl Marx's theory, as explicated in *Capital*, remains a central point for such discussions. By placing the reproduction of class society at the heart of his analysis, a focus on work, ownership, power, inequality, stratification, and socially induced dependency follows naturally. For Marx, the production of a surplus and the control over its utilization were central to the division of society into social classes. Only two classes are key to these core processes, both economically in terms of how the system functions and politically in terms of its possible future. That the fit between Marx's economic analyses and the sociological analysis of the population is not always obvious, speaks to the complexity of the market economy.

While Marx focused on the production of wealth, the social sciences are concerned with its distribution.[26] Income, education, power, and other factors that divide and segment the population become the critical variables. This warrants an additional focus on gender, race, ethnicity, and sexual orientation, all of which are used in such a manner as to prevent a more equitable allocation of resources.[27]

Most difficult has been the attempt to describe social relations in a manner that captures both their fixedness and their fluidity in proportions that do not distort reality. Depending on whether we view society from the perspective of income or education, for instance, we can elaborate somewhat dissimilar understandings of how society is structured.

The differences are illustrated in Figures 2.3 and 2.4, each of which is based on the very same data. In Figure 2.3, income categories are broken down by educational level. In Figure 2.4, educational attainment is broken down by income levels, whereby the five income categories each represent one-fifth of the population (as quintiles).

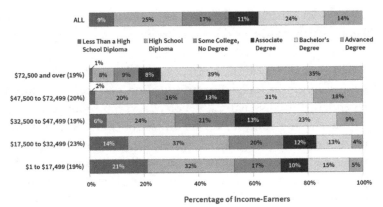

Figure 2.3   Income, by education level

Source: Sandy Baum, Charles Kurose, and Jennifer Ma, "How College Shapes Lives: Understanding the Issues," http://trends.collegeboard.org, October 2013, p. 26. Data derived from U.S. Census Bureau, 2012, Person income tables 2011: PINC-03. Reproduced with permission: The College Board.

Of note in Figure 2.3 is the heavy clustering towards the bottom left. High school graduates are a disproportionate share of the lower-income groups. A similar cluster exists at the upper right, where advanced degree and bachelor's degree holders dominate the upper tiers of society. This diagram shows a society that is both polarized towards the corners and also fractured at all levels by educational attainment.

Figure 2.4 sorts the population by educational level. Viewed this way, the clustering effect is greatly enhanced on the upper level by the importance of advanced, post-baccalaureate education and on the lower level by those with "less than a high school diploma." Society, from this vantage point, is more highly polarized. The middle rungs of the chart, however, project a series of equally sized groups along the axes representing "associate's degree" recipients and those with "some college, no degree."

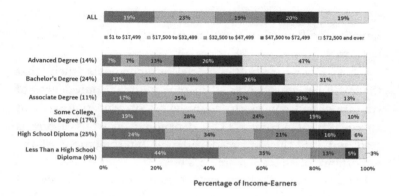

Figure 2.4   Education, by income level[28]

Source: Sandy Baum, Charles Kurose, and Jennifer Ma, "How College Shapes Lives,"
p. 25. Data derived from U.S. Census Bureau, 2012, Person income tables 2011:
PINC-03. Reproduced with permission The College Board.

As a result, education is more evenly dispersed among the
different income groups (Figure 2.4) than income among the
different educational groups (Figure 2.3). Underemployed
college graduates are part of the reason. They inhabit a world
educationally that does not have a counterpart in the sphere of
remuneration.

The charts demonstrate the limits of education in still
another important manner. For substantial portions of the
population, education is not destiny. In Figure 2.3, one-fourth
of the upper-income tier has less than a baccalaureate, one in
eleven at best a high school diploma. This attests to the ability
to succeed handsomely in life without the benefit of a formal
education beyond adolescence. And even though 80 percent
of the lowest tier have two-year associate's degrees or less, the
remaining one in five has a four-year degree or more, attesting
to the uselessness of education as a guarantee of social standing.
Even with graduate degrees, as seen in Figure 2.4, one out of

fourteen (7 percent) wind up in the bottom-income tier. The same is true for one in eight (12 percent) of the baccalaureate holders.[29]

Class society reshuffles social arrangements such that there can be equivalences of income without equivalences of education, and conversely, equivalences of education without an equality of incomes. Thus, depending on which figure is read and *how* they are read, different interpretations of the importance of education are possible.

Figures 2.3 and 2.4 both confirm education's importance and minimize its significance, just as in reality people can believe that education is key to success or that success is possible without excessive amounts of it. Both perspectives find confirmation. For the 26 percent of the elite who hold an associate's degree or less and the 20 percent of the lowest-income quintile with either a bachelor's or graduate degree, education has not been a decisive factor.

Class by definition

Some analysts rely on education as a marker of social standing, even though education has been and continues to be devalued, as underemployed college graduates can attest. Anthony P. Carnevale and Jeff Strohl, authors of many influential reports and publications, conclude that "in the postindustrial economy, educational attainment, in particular postsecondary educational attainment, has replaced the industrial concept of class as the primary marker for social stratification."[30]

Recent books echo this assessment. In his book *Labor's Love Lost: The Rise and Fall of the Working-Class Family in America* (2014), Andrew Cherlin writes, "in the post-1975 hourglass economy, I would claim, education, not occupation, is the best indicator of class position."[31] Tamar Draut, the author of *Sleeping Giant: How the New Working Class Will Transform America* (2016) similarly identifies education as key: "working class is defined as individuals in the labor force who do not have bachelor's degrees. This includes high school dropouts, high school graduates, people with some college, and associate's-degrees holders."[32]

Nevertheless, as we know, behind education lurks family background. Education is limited as a means to delineate social stratification among the populace. Substantial portions of the population experience upward mobility without the benefit of a college-level education or downward mobility even with it. When Draut acknowledges that "social scientists use three common methods to define class—by occupation, income, or education—and there is really no consensus about the 'right' way to do it," she might have said instead that none of the alternatives are quite accurate.[33] Through the use of criteria like these, part of reality goes missing.

A composite approach, using all three of these variables, takes us closer to the real world. Kevin Leicht and Scott Fitzgerald in *Middle Class Meltdown in America* (2014) define the middle class as those "who earn incomes approximately between $40,000 and $80,000 annually, who work as upper- and lower-level managers, professionals, and small business owners, who graduated from or at least attended a four-year college, and whose primary source of wealth is homeownership."[34]

Here too, though, many people only partially fit these criteria. Why is the lower limit for middle-class income $40,000, rather than, say, $33,500. And what about family size? Is a six-person household with a combined income of $40,000 as "middle class" as a single person with the same income. What about situations that fit more than one category? How does one label a family, for instance, in which the college-educated wife works in a "middle-class" profession such as accounting, but the husband, who never finished his degree, is employed part-time at minimal wages as a school crossing guard?

Definitions, by definition, miss the nuances and ambiguities that define life socioeconomically. One student commented that upward mobility for her and her siblings meant attending a different church than their parents, a church in which English rather than Spanish was the lingua franca. This type of social transformation is nowhere captured in the data.

As a lived experience, class is quite complicated. That income levels for many people are highly volatile from year to year also speaks against fixed taxonomies. Most definitions of class apply a limited set of categories in order to keep matters simple and intelligible, but they wind up distorting the circumstances that people actually live through. In essence, the attempt to simplify reality in order to make it understandable becomes part of the general process of mystification that fogs social relationships.

The closer to reality that these typologies get, the more complicated they become. Earl Wysong, Robert Perrucci, and David Wright, authors of *The New Class Society: Goodbye American Dream?* (2014) define classes "as collectivities of individuals and families with comparable amounts of four forms of economic and social resources, or forms of capital: investment, consumption, skill, and social capital." These produce two major classes—"the privileged class and the new working class"—as well as "five class segments that are clusters of people who share similar occupational characteristics and organizational affiliations that link them to similar levels of the four forms of capital."

Underemployed college graduates thus belong to the "contingent class segment" of "wage earners" who comprise

44–46 percent of the population and "work for wages in clerical and sales jobs, personal services, and transportation as truck drivers, clerks and machine operators. Members of this group are often college graduates. Incomes at $40K and lower."

The next "comfort class segment" (14–16 percent of the population) isn't quite appropriate for them: "Nurses, teachers, civil servants, very-small business owner, and skilled/unionized workers such as machinists or electricians. Incomes in the $40–$80K range but little investment capital."[35]

Other researchers focus instead on median income and the division of the population into equally sized groups (quintiles, for example). The simpler the model, the easier it becomes to identify socioeconomic trends. The problem, however, is that the dividing lines between groups rarely correspond with major fault lines within society. Researchers can easily follow trends for families within the 20–40 percent bracket of the income distribution hierarchy, yet in reality, it might be those in the 12–37 percent realm that face a particular set of economic and social circumstances.

In sum, theory helps us to understand basic issues such as why society is structured into social classes in the first place and why it evolves in such uncomplimentary and unaccommodating ways, as with underemployed college graduates. Empirical data provides highly specific information about many aspects of social life, but always at the cost of arbitrary distinctions, huge blind spots regarding nuance and ambiguity, and an inability to portray a system constantly in motion. In the next chapter, we examine education and class historically in an attempt to overcome some of these limits and deficiencies.

3

Class in transition:
historical background

Government involvement in higher education has followed the trajectory that characterizes development within society at large. Federal, state, and local governments only ventured into educational areas that were of little or no interest to the private sector as avenues of investment but which nonetheless were key to economic growth. Governmental bodies were careful to complement rather than supplant privately owned or privately endowed educational endeavors. Paul Mattick, whose *Marx and Keynes: The Limits of the Mixed Economy* (1969) remains the deepest exploration of government involvement in economic activity, notes that "government is therefore predominantly concerned with goods and services that have no place in the market, that is, with public works and public expenditures of all descriptions."[1]

The upper-class model of education, developed in colonial times with its private tutors, residential academies, and elite regional colleges that relied on wealthy benefactors, had limited applicability to the rapidly expanding farming, business, and urban sectors. Tuition-driven institutions have never been a viable model at any level of the income spectrum. Land grants, property taxes, and publicly issued bonds were the means to fund education on a wider basis in the mid-1800s, not only expanding it as a system but also extending its reach to new layers of the population. Much, much later came tuition payments and student loans to broaden the system even farther.

The state universities (land-grant institutions) that were established during the second half of the 1800s were molded with these various parameters in mind. Their primary foci were the humanities, social sciences, and agriculture-related disciplines, each area for its own separate reason. The humanities replicated the educational model in place at the elite colleges and were thought to benefit society in terms of citizenship, patriotism, and leadership skills. The social sciences, such as economics, sociology, and psychology, were cutting-edge fields that accompanied the demographic and business transformations then sweeping the country. These were viewed in managerial terms, as accompaniments to the elite vision of society propagated by the humanities.

The main economic driver, however, was the agriculture-related disciplines.[2] Basic research was key, especially for the newly developing chemical, food processing, and transportation industries. That the farming community benefitted directly from the dissemination of scientific findings also made the universities popular and important centers of commercial development.

The publicly financed institutions focused on mass education, deliberately avoiding competition with the small liberal arts colleges, many of them religiously based, that proliferated during this era. The latter appealed to elite families who could afford the steep rates for tuition, fees, and room and board, or to local gentries who preferred protective environments for their children.

If publicly funded institutions filled a void that the private sector had neglected, they also intervened when privately funded education collapsed. This was the situation in advanced professional education, especially in law, medicine, engineering, and education. By the early 1900s, the private sector was in retreat because these types of schools were expensive to sponsor and required highly trained and experienced faculty, and because the private sector had difficulty providing the requisite quality and depth of training. As the privately owned institutions closed, the publicly funded ones took their place, often through mergers and buy-outs.

In the post-World War II era, higher education emerged as a preferred venue for government spending precisely because it did not compete with the private sector. Education has always been treated as a type of infrastructure, along with roads and bridges. This remains true today. Training programs, particularly at the two-year colleges, have been especially popular with local businesses. Their need for trained personnel is insatiable, due to typically low wages and high turnover and because they need employees who possess appropriate certifications and licenses. The four-year schools, on the other hand, prepare students for administrative and technical work within the business, government, and nonprofit sectors.

Educational institutions are also economic engines, with acute importance in poor or isolated communities. They provide jobs, and they infuse the local economy with resources because of the services and supplies on which they depend. They are routinely considered part of the "spoils system" that characterizes the political world.

Each level of education relies on a separate combination of funding sources. Primary and secondary school systems depend heavily on local property taxes. This generally means active participation of property-owning parents, when they join in at all, in the functioning of the schools. The two-year colleges, however, derive much of their funding from state, county, and sometimes city governments and thus are responsible to a wider set of local and regional business and political interests. The public four-year colleges, for their part, are supported by the state and federal governments, and this often bestows a certain political independence, given how diffuse influence can be at that level.

These sets of interlocking and also competing alliances, from parents to corporations, help explain why higher education has expanded so rapidly and so consistently for such a long period of time. Despite the frequent exhortations to curtail spending and reduce taxes over the past decades, enrollments in post-secondary degree-granting institutions in 2016 stood at 19,841,014, compared to 15,312,289 in 2000.[3]

Coordination also remains difficult, not just between sectors and regions, but within each of them as well. On the collegiate level alone, there are 2,395 four-year and 1,500 two-year institutions. These in turn can be divided into public (1,583), private nonprofit (1,392), and private for-profit (920) institutions. On the elementary and secondary levels, over 13,000 separate school districts preside over aspects of the curriculum, schedule, and personnel. When government, regional, and independent charter schools and agencies are added, the total reaches 18,243 jurisdictional bodies.[4]

This is why, too, federal and state officials often entice compliance with new rules and directives through extra funding, since legally they are powerless to assert themselves. In order to disburse federal financial aid, for instance, collegiate institutions must comply with a host of regulations concerning campus safety, anti-discriminatory measures, and athletics.

The development of for-profit institutions in recent times has not changed any of these dynamics. For-profit schools, despite their ability to pick selectively the geographic and educational areas they enter, are almost entirely dependent on government largesse; even more, the for-profit sector is mainly a government creation. On average, 72 percent of their revenues derive from the loans and grants that various government agencies award to individual students; at some schools, it is 90 percent, the legal maximum.[5]

The government has encouraged the growth of for-profit institutions as a means of cost containment, although the strategy has backfired because so many of these institutions have substandard records in terms of retention, graduation, and placement. When ITT Educational Services declared bankruptcy in 2015, after it was charged with predatory student lending, and its ability to issue federal financial aid to students was revoked, it closed 130 sites, affecting 35,000 students and 8,000 employees. At Corinthian Colleges, whose misdeeds included the misrepresentation of job-placement rates, false and predatory advertising, securities fraud, and more, the final round of closures left 16,000 students without a means to complete their programs.[6] The scale alone is unprecedented. To put matters in perspective: during the 2016–17 academic year, 112 institutions of higher education closed, of which 92 were for-profit and 20 non-profit.[7]

Meanwhile, a particularly odd dynamic has overtaken the publicly funded institutions, which require huge subsidies in order to function. As government support declines, they have resorted to tuition hikes and other forms of revenue-enhancement to overcome the shortfalls. Between 2008 and 2013, state funding for higher education declined 28 percent per student, while tuition at four-year public colleges rose 27 percent in response.[8] This constitutes an odd form of privatization. In effect, these institutions are being sold off in installment-fashion by charging their "customers" higher prices.

The students (and their parents) don't actually become owners, even though their payments make possible the reduction in government subsidies.

No mention of anything like this can be found in economics textbooks, so unprecedented is the situation and so unlike anything that existing economic models can account for. There is a strange irony in the entire situation, whereby public institutions are quasi-privatized at a moment when the relationship between higher education and social mobility has collapsed. Just the opposite situation prevailed a century before, when failing privately owned educational enterprises were incorporated into the public sector because higher education had become an increasingly important factor in economic development.

Education and mobility

Prior to World War II, only about half of all children finished high school, and only about a third of high school graduates continued on to college. Of the 18–24 year-olds, this represented less than 10 percent (compared to 40 percent today).[9] Society in general was highly segregated in terms of occupations and social class.[10]

Farming occupations were en route to their near-extinction, having declined from half of the workforce around 1870 to a third of that level by 1940. Huge increases in productivity, fostered by the publicly funded universities, had been instrumental in this transformation. Blue-collar occupations comprised nearly 40 percent of all employment, on a par with other nations similarly involved in the first wave of industrial development. To note, too, is that the industrial proletariat did not represent a majority of employees. In terms of class consciousness, this would prove to be important.

The service occupations, at nearly 30 percent of the workforce, caused considerable confusion. By the late 1800s, labor organizers were already casting a wary eye at their growing presence within the economy. Service occupations were considered secondary to the primary focus of the capitalist economy; they were regarded as a late-developing phenomenon that encompassed fields peripheral to the core enterprises of modern society. Service workers were thoroughly working class, to be sure, but they were not productive workers who manufactured commodities.

That the service occupations included large numbers of female employees further confused existing models of class composition, since they implied a frame of reference in which strict divisions between male and female, and manufacturing and service industries, were blurred. It was difficult to organize unions in these areas, which likewise reinforced the prevailing prejudices.

College-educated individuals were employed as managers, officials, and professionals, areas that were growing in overall numbers within the workforce. By 1940, they already equaled the proportion still involved in agriculture. The college-educated lived visibly distant from everyone else in terms of residential districts, social and interpersonal activities, and the breadth and extent of their consumer purchases. They were clearly a social class unto themselves, even though they functioned economically as intermediaries between the upper and lower classes.

"Middle class," explains Steve Fraser, is a "slippery category, one that has always had vaguely defined boundaries":

Once it seemed intended to encompass small property-holders and assorted professionals. Then it came to embrace people doing white-collar work at the mid-levels of corporate and government bureaucracies with a certain amount of education and skilled manual or technical knowledge. With the advent of mass consumption capitalism, "middle class" came to mean mainly, although not only, a certain material standard of living—that is, a category of consumption rather than work.[11]

Notions of "middle class" underwent multiple redefinitions, something that has been true during the entire history of industrialization, including today.

Simultaneous with these early to mid-twentieth-century developments, the relationship between education and class emerged as an alternative understanding of this same set of issues. A high school diploma was the important educational credential as far as most people were concerned, with college reserved for members of the elite.

High school graduates were heavily clustered in "industries that produced high technology and recently innovated goods, such as aircraft, business machinery, and scientific and photographic equipment." These industries "used continuous-process and batch technologies to a greater degree than did other industries, and these industries included petroleum refining, dairy products, paints and varnishes, and nonferrous metals."[12] In other words, cutting-edge industries employed higher concentrations of high school-educated workers than did other areas of the economy.

These new and dynamic sectors also tended to be capital-intensive. They relied on electricity as a power source to an unprecedented degree, an example of the ripple effects of productivity gains when they occur in key infrastructural areas. Similar processes had been at work with the steam engine at the beginning of the industrial era, the railroad that accompanied the build-out of heavy industry in the late 1800s, the automobile and roadway system during the mid-twentieth century, and the Internet today.

In the United States during the first half of the twentieth century, continuous-process manufacturing referred to products that required little assembly, such as food products, paper, and soap. Batch processing referred to liquid, semi-solid, and gaseous matter, such as in the chemical, dairy, and molten metal industries. Thus, over 40 percent of the employees in the printing and publishing, petroleum refining, and electrical machinery industries had high school diplomas, but fewer than 20 percent were so educated in many textile and construction fields.

Similar educational dichotomies prevailed in the service industry. Within the banking field, for instance, virtually every job required a high school diploma, something not at all true for the food industry. Newer and older technologies were divided by educational level.

* * *

Higher education remained a relatively minor feature of society until the great expansion of the government sector after World War II. If the economic Depression of the 1930s had interfered with people's ability to discern long-term transformations within society at large, the world wars that preceded and then followed the Depression had shown the efficacy of government spending as a means to stimulate the economy.[13]

After World War I, nonetheless, the federal government retreated from active economic involvement. The 1920s, consequently, were scarred by recessions and stock market speculation. Since no one desired a return to the 1920s or the 1930s, government funding for an expanded educational sector became a means to replicate the types of economic successes that had been possible as wartime measures. As World War II wound down and armaments expenditures were reduced, outlays for education took on a new importance.

The G.I. Bill of 1944 (Servicemen's Readjustment Act) was counterintuitive from several perspectives. For one, the majority of veterans did not bother with its educational benefits. Of those who did, more than two-thirds used them for "agricultural," "on the job," or "below college" programs. The latter were the kinds of occupational training programs that today are found at two-year and for-profit trade schools. The remainder of students, some 2¼ million out of 16 million eligible veterans, enrolled in college, primarily in the liberal arts but also in fields that had become parts of the publicly funded higher education system, such as engineering, education, medicine and dentistry, and the sciences.[14]

College enrollments were boosted by some 75 percent during the late 1940s, much of this the result of pent-up demand. Surveys of recipients confirmed that the overwhelming majority of those who attended college would have attended even if the war had not intervened.[15] The G.I. Bill, though, provided living stipends, tuition, fees, books, and supplies, a comprehensive approach to financial aid that helped transform attendance patterns. As students, veterans were older and often married. As college graduates, they entered the labor force as highly literate, skilled, motivated, appreciative of government benefits, and oriented towards professional, administrative, and entrepreneurial careers. They also entered an economy that expanded quickly because of the ongoing infusion of governmental resources.

The G.I. Bill sharpened everyone's ideas about the relationship between education and class. Many veterans had drawn class-oriented conclusions about education during the war, since college attendance was "one of the major criteria used by the Armed Forces to sort soldiers from officers."[16] The veterans, subsequently, focused their attention not on their own careers, which were already predetermined class-wise, but on the fate of their children. The latter came of age starting in the 1950s, but especially during the 1960s, when for the first time there was a discernible working-class presence in higher education.

Government—business—education

The post-war world that emerged in the late 1940s was altogether different from the world that people had known before. The war had accelerated the pace of change, both economically and socially. Between 1950, by which time the economy had begun to stabilize, and 1970, the nation's population expanded by 35 percent. This was the heyday of the Keynesian era, when it was thought that government spending could be increased with few detrimental effects on the economy at large.[17] Population growth, as rapid as it was, actually lagged behind other crucial indicators of prosperity, a surefire sign that opportunities were opening for a wider segment of society.

During those decades, the number of collegiate institutions also grew by 35 percent. If 80,000 professors were hired between 1946 and 1950—an increase of 50 percent in four years' time, nearly 200,000 faculty positions were created over the next twenty years.[18] The number of college students swelled exponentially, more than tripling during that same time frame. An additional 5,639,000 students were absorbed into the postsecondary system. The years 1960–70 (in bold in Table 3.1) were pivotal in terms of growth.

Table 3.1 The expansion of higher education

Year	Population (in millions)	Postsecondary institutions*	Enrollments (in thousands)*	Percent of 18–24 year-olds
1940	132.1	1708	1494	9.1
1945	139.9	1768	2078	12.5
1950	151.7	1863	2281	14.2
1955	165.3	1850	2918	19.5
1960	180.7	1959	3583	22.2
1965	194.3	2230	5928	27.7
1970	204.9	2525	7920	32.1

Source: U.S. Census Bureau, *Historical Statistics of the United States: Colonial Times to 1970, Parts 1–2*, www.census.gov, Tables: A: 6; H: 689, 696, 700–701, 706–707.
*=1946/1956/1966, 30 July 2015.

Colleges and universities grew larger in size and scope to accommodate the influx; campuses and classrooms everywhere were flooded with students.

Higher education had become mass education to an unprecedented degree. Richard B. Freeman, whose pioneering book *The Overeducated American* documented underemployment among college students during that era, calculated that "the number of workers with at least one year of college training surpassed both the number of union members and the number of manufacturing production workers in the mid-1960s, substantially altering the nature of the American labor market." By 1970, a larger number of people were employed in collegiate-related occupations than in either the automobile or steel industries.[19]

Suddenly, college students were a recognizable constituency. Their political attitudes, preferred lifestyles, and tastes in music and food became topics of interest within adjacent sectors of society, in particular, for the media, advertisers, and politicians. By 1970, one of every three 18–24 year-olds was enrolled in a collegiate institution of some sort. That "twenty percent of employed male and female graduates ... ended up in areas 'not related' to their college studies" also drew attention.[20] Society had changed quite rapidly, as had its social and class compositions.

Government spending, of course, meant additional layers of administrators to manage and monitor expenditures. Government-funded employment doubled between 1950 and 1970, from just over 6 million to 12½ million. Even though attention has focused on the federal level, the overwhelming majority of new employees were appointed by state and local funding entities. These two lower levels of government accounted for over three-fourths of all government employees. They also expanded more than three times as quickly as the federal government during these two decades.[21]

Everywhere, there was more government per person, especially on the local levels that people interacted with frequently. Employment in education was the largest subgroup of governmental employees, with public school teachers the major component. Funding for higher education also expanded faster than the economy at large and two-year colleges even faster than four-year ones.[22]

The business world underwent a complementary transformation. Its expansion, both domestically and internationally, accompanied ever-higher levels of production and productivity. Mechanization alone added entirely new levels of complexity to operating procedures. Needed as well was the wherewithal to distribute, market, and sell goods on an unprecedented scale. All these functions required modernized bureaucracies. White-collar (office) positions increased by 75 percent, even though the civilian labor force only increased by one-third:

Table 3.2 The expansion of the workforce (in thousands)

	1950	*1970*	*Percent of increase*
Total population	151,700	204,900	35%
Civilian labor force	59,230	80,603	36%
Manual workers	24,266	29,169	20%
Service workers	6,180	10,251	66%
White-collar employees	21,601	37,857	75%

Source: U.S. Census Bureau, *Historical Statistics of the United States*, D: pp. 182–183, 188, 193, July 30, 2015.

The workforce within the United States was changing. Over the period 1950–70, white-collar professions overtook traditional manual occupations and accounted for nearly half of all employment nationwide.

Meanwhile, blue-collar jobs had declined to little more than a third of all employment. Farming, with only 4 percent of the workforce, virtually disappeared from the lexicon of sustainable professions.[23] Keep in mind, too, that these broad categories often concealed as much as they seemed to clarify. The white-collar workforce, for instance, was split evenly between professional and managerial positions on the one side and clerical and sales occupations on the other, a bifurcated service world that became one of the hallmarks of the modern age.[24]

The dual needs of governing and commerce were reflected in the growth of higher education—more college students, a heavy emphasis on occupational training at the two-year colleges and the liberal arts at the four-year schools, a stronger governmental presence especially on the local and state levels as reflected in the educational system, and a shift towards service and office (white-collar) work, much of which required higher levels of schooling than before. "The diploma," according to Richard

Vedder, became a "screening device" that allowed "businesses to narrow down the applicant pool quickly and almost without cost to the employer."[25] Government and business worked in tandem to shape the world of work, using the educational system as the conduit.

Government spending, business expansion, the growth of the service and white-collar sectors, and the build-out of higher education precipitated the reshuffling of social classes. Because each area had mushroomed more quickly than the population, opportunities developed across a broad range of areas.

Class consumption

The immediate post-World War II decades marked a turning point in working-class history. For the first time, working-class families were able to purchase a wide variety of non-perishable and durable goods, such as kitchen appliances and automobiles, conveniences that until then had been mostly confined to the middle and upper classes. The urban infrastructure of electricity, piped water, and indoor toilets—largely completed before the war—opened many possibilities. By 1970, refrigerators and washing machines were owned by virtually all households. Half had ranges in their kitchens and a clothes dryer; many also had a dishwasher. Televisions were ubiquitous, and air conditioning was making its appearance in people's homes and automobiles.[26]

The increase in personal and familial consumption also helped alter the social class configuration that had emerged initially with industrialization. Income was key. Each new purchase conferred convenience and status, advantages exhibited both privately and publicly.

Mass consumption in the modern sense of manufactured commodities begins with the middle classes, if only because productivity gains occur piecemeal and commodity prices remain relatively high for an extended period of time. Middle- and upper-income individuals also have the financial wherewithal to purchase the latest iterations of new products. To be on the cutting edge of consumption is to exist within a moment of time that is temporary and fleeting. Improved products follow in rapid order. In recent times, iPods, e-books, iPads, tablets, and iPhones, each in multiple iterations, created an ever-changing array of new possibilities, with each level embodying a higher level of functionality.

Product development renders machines and gadgets obsolete before they are worn out physically; in other words, the competitive process is destructive in terms of material objects and resources. Market stabilization occurs when a high degree of monopolization overtakes a particular productive sphere. If there are sufficient barriers to new business entrants, then the rate of innovation slows. Product differentiation (variations in models, colors, accessories, etc.) replaces product innovation.

As consumption trickles down, class boundaries tend to blur. What had been the domain of the upper classes becomes the domain of the middle and working classes as well. Over time, what were once perceived as luxuries are now regarded as necessities, and all of society is portrayed as if it is a single entity. With mass consumption, the bourgeois mode of life becomes the norm. It is this conception of reality that drives the marketing and advertising industries.

That lower-class consumption often involves items more shoddily built, less functional, and less attractive does not negate the overall trends. The variability of models, colors, and extra features—all of which are calibrated to distinct income levels—means that consumption is stratified, when not altogether individualized. Clothing had evolved along these lines for some decades already. Supermarkets offered thousands of items, sorted by brand, size, and price. Department stores and malls presented analogous displays of goods. Small retail outlets proliferated.

Notwithstanding the tremendous advances in productivity in the immediate post-war period, enhanced consumption presupposed better pay and stable employment. Andrew Cherlin, who has plotted the fate of the working-class family in great detail, summarizes the era as one in which "the fortunes of the working-class family crested during the thirty-year period that followed World War II." He explains that "incomes rose sharply and prosperity spread more broadly than ever before. The average manufacturing wage more than doubled in purchasing power from 1950 to 1970."[27]

All this signified a form of upward mobility, irrespective of actual wage levels. Whether someone was truly a member of the middle class seemed not to matter when it came to consumption and the choices it offered. These product innovations also lightened women's toil in particular, relieving them of the need to make one's own clothing, food shop daily, and spend long hours cooking. Consumption transformed the family, which in turn prompted a wide host of vital social changes.

Consumption offered a partial escape from the years of scarcity that had characterized the Depression of the 1930s and the dreariness of the war years that followed. Working-class life had been an unfortunate existence, with harsh living conditions, overcrowded dwellings, slums, insufficient income, limited possibilities for alternative employment or upward mobility, long and unpleasant commutes on crowded systems of public transportation, and deadening, repetitive, unchallenging jobs. While highly skilled workers carved out relatively stable lives, the majority of the working class had been stuck in place. However, the everyday sameness of life seemed to be coming to an end.

Even the labor movement thought in terms of transcending working-class existence by means of higher wages and improved working conditions. Radical organizations took these notions a further step, since a socialist society would have no need to maintain class divisions. For them the eradication of capitalism meant the disappearance of the negative conditions that characterized working-class life. Post-war prosperity offered to nearly everybody what had been on their minds already, albeit in a manner not anticipated by anyone.

Meanwhile, the world of work had also undergone a process of individuation that likewise downplayed the emphasis on social class as an identity marker. Major sectors of the economy, both blue and white collar, introduced minute differences in titles and pay scales as a means to keep employees in competition with one another while also providing a small measure of occupational and income flexibility.[28] Underneath executive managers were department managers, unit managers, deputy managers, associate managers, assistant managers, and so on, throughout all occupations and professions.

The borders that had for a century separated the lower echelons of the elite from the remainder of the population had been broached in terms of the nature of employment (white-collar work), places of residence (home ownership and suburbia), and consumption. Education, specifically a college education, added a new dimension to this opening. For a portion of the working class, education became a vehicle for upward mobility. To be college educated meant that you were part of the middle class. Randall Collins echoed widely accepted sentiments when he wrote that "education is the most important determinant yet discovered of how far one will go in today's world."[29]

Richard Sennett and Jonathan Cobb, astute observers of this transition, commented in *The Hidden Injuries of Class* (1972) that "in terms of income, amount of taxing physical exertion, and styles of living, the lines are not now sharp between many blue-collar and low-level office workers." They added, however, "to conclude that class differences are therefore disappearing would be wrong." Instead, "the lines of class difference are being redrawn."[30]

Class and consciousness

If the massive production of consumption items aimed at all levels of the income hierarchy blurred class divisions, the public's understanding of class identity was also influenced by a discussion that emanated from within the academic world but was transmitted to the general public by the media. The best-known print example of this genre of thinking was Daniel Bell's *The End of Ideology* (1960) because of its popularity among academics and college students. Much later, André Gorz's *Farewell to the Working Class* (1980) provided a radical rather than a liberal perspective.[31] Newspaper journalists, radio hosts, and television news anchors, however, were the primary conduits to these dialogues for the working class.

These commentaries, taken collectively, represented an intense ideological barrage on working-class identity. They were also accompanied by interpretive discussion regarding the disappearance of the working class and of social classes altogether. Yet even without this sociopolitical overlay, the sheer volume of dialogue set the parameters within which social class was dissected. The working class was encouraged to view itself as something other than what it was, that is, to think of itself as a sort of middle class in training. Of note, too, is that neither the business world nor the government were much involved or interested in these developments. Instead, the college-educated middle class was paraded as worthy of emulation, as the model for the lower ranks of society in terms of education and status. Both the bourgeoisie and the working class disappeared from sight.

Class identity become complicated and problematic.[32] It wasn't so much that working-class consciousness disappeared in the post-war era as that people submerged their working-class identities. This was true even for those parts of the population that remained ensconced in traditionally working-class occupations, neighborhoods, and incomes. To self-identify as working class was to reveal yourself as rooted in the present, rather than living for the future.

Class transformation, in any case, was focused on children, not on adults. Working-class parents were acutely aware of how their own educations and social advancement had been thwarted by the Depression, World War II, and the need to work. In other words, working-class parents raised their children to be middle class. In the process, they kept quiet about their own identities or even embraced the middle-class label, not only for the sake of their children but because white-collar work was available, home ownership became feasible (a prime benefit of the G.I. Bill, at least for the white segments of the population),[33] and the general level of consumption blurred class differentials.

In the post-war era, substantial portions of the working class thought of themselves in dual class terms, as the working-class parents of middle-class children or as college graduates from working-class backgrounds. College officials eventually referred to the latter as "first generation" students, a description that already by 1958 fit over half (53.1 percent) of all college students.[34] The class composition of college students had altered rapidly. In effect, parts of the working class had been invited to join the upper orders of society.

The result was a bifurcated working class. One part was absorbed into the middle class, while the remainder either did not recognize the importance of education as a lever of social mobility, or were prevented from taking advantage of it. These tended to be parts of the working class whose agrarian roots were quite recent and who were segregated along racial, ethnic, and geographical divisions. The non-collegiate portion of the working class would soon be swept away by deindustrialization—that is, the wholesale transformation of the remaining working class into the working poor.

The seeming disappearance of the working class and the concomitant reorientation of class consciousness—for example, its partial eradication—set the stage for the emergence of a host of alternate identities. Class had never been an exclusive marker of identity in any case, but simply one of many variables that were based on one's parents and partners: their ethnicity and race, religious adherence, geographic background, nationality at birth, current occupation, home community, and more.

The "identity politics" of the last few decades have their roots in the dissolution of the working class in the post-war era. Gender and sexual orientation added still other modes of self-definition. Identity was a negotiation in which individuals deployed hyphenated and multiple self-descriptions in new ways, no longer to affirm the "Americanization" of immigrants, for example, as "Italian-American." These altered ways of thinking about identity emerged during the 1960s, led by the racial minority that had faced unrelenting hostility, discrimination, and aggression. The adoption of "African American" and "black" threw into sharp relief the "melting pot" ideology that had applied solely to the white immigrant communities of European origin.

A half century ago, the confusion over class helped open the general public to new attitudes about diversity. As women and minorities joined the paid workforce in greater numbers, they prompted a major reassessment of accepted truths about society's homogeneity. Positive or negative reactions largely hinged on how one viewed the future. In other words, cultural reorientation was a by-product of upward mobility. For those not so lucky, these same factors regarding race, ethnicity, and gender could easily be perceived as precipitating their own downward mobility.

Analysts of social class had the greatest difficulty sorting through these various levels of class consciousness and class ambiguity, just as we have seen in the last chapter the difficulties they have had in differentiating one social class from the next. On the one side were authors like Daniel Bell and André Gorz, who tended to erase the past. For Gorz, "the neo-proletariat is no more than a vague area made up of constantly changing individuals whose main aim is not to seize power in order to build a new world, but to regain power over their own lives by disengaging from the market rationality of productivism."[35] His metaphors are key: a "vague area" of "constantly changing individuals" who act by "disengaging."

On the other side were authors such as Studs Terkel, whose collections of interviews reaffirmed the continued relevance of a working-class identity, or scholars such as Reeve Vanneman and Lynn Weber Cannon, whose *The American Perception of Class* (1987) charted several decades of sociological surveys and came to similar conclusions. Their book opened with a dilemma: "conventional wisdom tells us that Americans are not class conscious."[36] Which was it—class identity as no longer relevant, or class identity as effervescent as ever? A huge literature was produced.

Popular culture, on the other hand, tended to be much less constrained. Several long-playing television shows depicted the working class in all its contradictions. The sitcom, *All In The Family*, ran for nine seasons during the 1970s.[37] Father figure and lead character Archie Bunker embodied a rigid, tough-talking, and patriarchal conservatism that was laced with an implicit racism and scoffed at everything unfamiliar. His long-haired, college-attending son-in-law absorbed the brunt of Bunker's acerbic wit, while their wives (mother and daughter) transgressed class boundaries, in the mother's case by means of a stereotyped ignorance that masked unacknowledged skill and insight. Class, race, and gender were presented within a complex and contradictory reality.

A second show, *The Jeffersons*, depicted an upwardly mobile African American family. Like *All In The Family*, the older male character was presented as a caricature, too witty and smart to be as uninformed as he was. His relationship with his college-attending son, however, was warm and supportive. And rather than representing class as a polarizing factor, as had *All in the Family*, *The Jeffersons* showed how class was subsumed within racial and cultural dynamics. Friends and family represented a broad spectrum of individuals who spanned the dividing line that supposedly separated the middle from the working class.

These shows were products of the 1970s. Their creator, Norman Lear, was groundbreaking in his treatment of social issues, a far cry from the bland, happy and white families of the previous decade. But his main characters functioned on the level of caricature, nasty in one case, full of bombast in the other. Lear seemed to assume that exposure to life's complexities would lead audiences in the direction of greater racial and gender tolerance. Such an approach may have also had an unintended effect of encouraging people to function in public in ways not entirely consonant with their inner beliefs and doubts. By not confronting reality head-on, this approach risked becoming another moment of silencing, in which issues are acknowledged without ever being fully resolved.

A third show, *Law and Order*, aired for two full decades beginning in 1990. It exhibited a greater subtlety and sophistication in the treatment of social class, in part because by then the working class no longer needed to be referenced explicitly. Times had changed. This show used drama rather than comedic repartee to confront reality.

The lead figure in *Law and Order* was the assistant district attorney, Jack McCoy, whose never-seen police officer father attested to his working-class roots. McCoy represented liberal New York, yet because of his background he could talk tough to street detectives like Lenny Briscoe. McCoy, in a word, had fluency both in the working class because of his upbringing and in the upper-middle class because of his law school education and lofty occupation. His ability to cross class boundaries helped bind the show into a cohesive whole.

The homicide detective, Lenny Briscoe, gives us still another image of the working class. Unlike *All In The Family* with its representation of the white working class as crude, sharp-tongued, and cynical, Briscoe's street-smarts' wit is combined with an ability for deep self-reflection (about his alcoholism and his ruined relationship with his daughter) and genuine compassion for other people's troubles. He is openly bothered by human suffering. Lennie Briscoe personifies the working class as the middle class hoped it would be.

* * *

Today, the fate of underemployed college graduates is once again shifting the definition and relevance of working-class identity. Employment fields that traditionally required a high school diploma are now crowded with college graduates. Among secretaries and administrative assistants in one survey, 30 percent listed a high school diploma as their highest degree and earned a median salary of $33,600. Another 15 percent listed a bachelor's degree and earned a median salary of $38,600. The salary differences among retail salespersons were more pronounced: the 31 percent with a high school diploma earned median salaries of $30,100, the 23 percent with a baccalaureate degree had median earnings of $45,000.[38]

Sociologists refer to the mismatch between employment and educational levels as "status inconsistency." Michael Hout calculates that perhaps a third of the population fits this definition. He also finds that how you ask people about class identification matters greatly, since "open-ended questions that do not prompt respondents with any answer categories get far more mentions of the middle class and far fewer mention of the working class."[39] This is another way of saying that the question anticipates the answer, a long-standing issue within the field of survey research.

Survey results, nevertheless, continue to show that people have well-defined notions of social status and their own respective positions within society, despite all that has been said about the loss of class identity. The clearest answers come when the three factors of income, occupation, and education are taken one at a time.[40] The overwhelming majority of employees (aged

25 and older) with family incomes above $75,000 consider themselves middle-class, whereas those earning under $50,000 predominately self-identify as working-class. "Lower"- and "upper"-class labels are chosen only by small subgroups, regardless of their level of income.

Similar dichotomies occur by occupational category. The majority of professionals, the self-employed (white collar), and managers identify as middle-class, whereas other white-collar employees, blue-collar employees (whether self-employed, skilled, or unskilled), farmers and agricultural workers, and low-wage service employees most often choose working class as the appropriate identifier. Here too, the lower- and upper-class descriptors are chosen by relatively few. Identification by education is as might be expected. The majority of college graduates identify as middle class, the majority of everyone else as working class, with lower- and upper-class identity lagging far behind.

In the decades following World War II, the partial absorption of the working class into a newly constituted middle class was one of capitalism's greatest achievements. After three-quarters of a century of full-scale industrialization, the economy was able to elevate parts of the working class to heights that had long been the preserve of their social betters. It had taken roughly the same amount of time, from the later decades of the 1800s until the post-war decades, for the agricultural population of the United States to be absorbed into the working and middle classes, although more often as victims rather than as beneficiaries of economic development.

This process is in reverse now. Parts of the middle class are being reabsorbed into the working class. Productivity gains over time have eliminated the social groups responsible for those gains in the first place. The fate of the industrial proletariat is no different from the fate of the agricultural population. The service sector is next.

The first inkling of the change in fortune for college graduates occurred during the 1970s, when they faced underemployment in crisis proportions.

4

Underemployment
through the decades

Underemployment and precarity are relatively new ways to think about dysfunction within the capitalist economy. They supplant the more traditional foci of poverty and unemployment, both of which are more serious in terms of their impacts on people's lives but less pervasive throughout society in general. In truth, these four categories—underemployment, precarity, poverty, and unemployment—define overlapping levels of socially induced misfortune.

Notwithstanding the 1950s' reputation for prosperity, underemployment for college graduates accompanied that era's build-out of the collegiate system. Two years post-graduation, 18 percent of the class of 1958 reported that a four-year degree was not necessary for the jobs they held.[1] The type of underemployment they faced, however, was different from the underemployment that developed in the decades that followed. That earlier period was characterized not by a lack of appropriate positions, but by a superabundance of them. Richard Freeman, whose *The Overeducated American* has been mentioned previously, used data from the U.S. Census Bureau and Department of Labor to calculate that there was a favorable ratio of 2.33 professional or managerial positions per graduate at the time.[2]

This would seem to favor college graduates, except that these positions were already occupied. For employers choosing between education and experience, the latter generally triumphed. Only when college graduates competed against similarly inexperienced non-graduates were they preferred. This presupposed positions that needed to be filled, due to retirements, or when incumbents left one position for a different one. For the college graduates, though, it was the great expansion of business and government in the post-war era that facilitated their incorporation into the workforce.

Over the next several decades, office work became synonymous with a college education, Simultaneously, the evening divisions of colleges and universities (commonly referred to as "night school") witnessed an infusion of part-time students.[3] Many of these students already held administrative positions in nearby corporate offices and government agencies, but they feared that career advancement or even further employment would hinge on possession of a college degree. For the preexisting workforce, returning to school was a hedge against the future.

If "the 1970s marked the last full decade when a large slice of the population didn't need a college degree," the upper echelons of society spent that time in a process of rapid re-credentialing.[4] By 1970, 45 percent of professional and managerial positions were held by college graduates, so rapid had been the changeover during the previous decade. By the late 1980s, employees with only a high school degree had been eliminated from wide swaths of the administrative world.

Issues of underemployment and precarity were also given new attention. For example, in the mid-1970s, the Bureau of Labor Statistics supplemented the unemployment rate with a half dozen other measures, the most extensive of which used a complicated formula that produced a considerably higher rate.[5] Thus, in 2011 in the aftermath of the Great Recession, there were 13.7 million unemployed, but also 8.6 million involuntary part-time employees ("available for full-time work") and 2.6 million marginally attached ("not looking for work but want and would take a job"). This added up to 15.9 percent of the labor force. In October 2018, while the official unemployment rate was 3.7 percent, the combined rate was double at 7.4 percent.[6]

The labor force participation rate (roughly, the percentage of adults available for work) provides another means to judge economic functioning. It hovered between 60–67 percent throughout the last decades of the twentieth century, and as of October 2018 was 62.9 percent.[7] With a potential labor force that today numbers some 160 million, slight changes in the labor force participation rate encompass significant numbers of people. Men, in particular, have experienced a steep decline of 10 percent since 1970.[8] And even though roughly two-thirds of the adult population are counted as part of the available workforce, we nonetheless do not have a good understanding of the remaining third, some of whom (for example, adolescents, retirees, homemakers) would be eager to participate in economic activity if suitable positions were available.[9]

Some of the most illuminating work on workforce utilization has been done by researchers who attempt to go beyond institutional boundaries. When Dean Morse's *The Peripheral Worker* was published in 1969, the country was just entering the severe period of economic turmoil that we now recognize as a landmark of the modern age. Morse scrutinized employees "who have had work experience of any kind other than full time for a full year." In other words, he identified the extent to which people had been subjected to part-time and limited-term employment, which he calculated at 44 percent in 1965, some 38 million out of a total of 86 million employees.[10] Similar amounts of underemployment had characterized the previous decade and a half.

David Livingston's *The Education-Jobs Gap* (1998) used an alternative measure of workplace underutilization. He explored the "discrepancy between our work-related knowledge" and "our opportunities to use this knowledge in interesting and fairly compensated work." Besides formal education, he included several measures commonly overlooked: on- and off-the-job training opportunities and other informal educational activities. According to his calculations, underemployment grew in importance from 46 percent of the workforce in 1972 to 62 percent in 1990.[11]

Because policy discussions tended to focus on poverty as the most critical social dynamic, underlying issues like underemployment and precarity needed to be rediscovered, as the economy began to stagnate in the late twentieth century. That the poverty rate had also declined dramatically during the prosperous decades following World War II—from 22.4 percent in 1959 to 11.1 percent in 1973—encouraged everyone to think of these sorts of issues as residual rather than fundamental.[12]

Re-industrialization

The reorganization of the economy during the late twentieth century set the stage in terms of the working conditions that confront college graduates today. Properly speaking, those decades ought to be known as a time of *re*-industrialization rather than *de*-industrialization. Everything about the world of work changed, and although the productive workforce eventually shrank in numbers, they produced more than ever.

As this transformation unfolded, it fooled most observers. In their widely influential *The Deindustrialization of America* (1982), Barry Bluestone and Bennett Harrison calculated that "somewhere between 32 and 38 million jobs were lost during the 1970s as the direct result of private disinvestment in American business."[13] Owners closed their factories or else moved them elsewhere, attracted by cheaper wages and fewer regulations. In *The Disposable American* (2007), Louis Uchitelle estimated that an additional 30 million jobs were cut during the last two decades of the century, some 7–8 percent annually.[14] Tumult defined the American economy. Capital investment in factories and machine tools was pegged at a lifespan of 7.1 years, so rapid was the turnover.[15]

What was left out of view in these alarming accounts was that manufacturing employment continued to expand during the 1970s despite the great turmoil, reaching a peak of 19.5 million employees in 1979. And while manufacturing employment declined somewhat by 2000, to 17.3 million, it was still higher than nearly every year during industrialization's heyday between 1950 and 1970, when it ranged between 14.1 to 17.9 million.[16]

How are we to understand these two sets of contradictory facts: on the one side, industrialization as comprehensive as ever, with fluctuations that tended toward the high side, and on the other, a turnover of personnel so rapid and all-encompassing that the entire workforce was replaced several times over?

Geography provides part of the answer. The United States was reindustrializing on a new footing, and industry and its employees were on the move. To a great extent, the historical centers of industrialization in the Northeast and Midwest were abandoned, while new production facilities were established in the South and the Southwest. By 1972, one-quarter of all manufacturing jobs were located in the southern regions of the country. Empty factories littered the Northeast and Midwest. Electronics and plastics manufacturing replaced metal production. Elsewhere, assembly plants had become as important economically as those processing raw materials.

The new factories looked different too. Gone were the multi-storied brick buildings with ample windows that had characterized the industrial era. A stripped-down architecture took its place, "big-box"-type constructions of one or two stories that sometimes included a few windows on upper-level corners for administrative offices. Factories, warehouses, distribution centers, and big-box retail establishments became indistinguishable when viewed from their exteriors. Economic reality took on an undifferentiated uniformity that blurred visual comprehension. The new workplace regime combined greater intensities of mechanization and automation with a wholesale disregard for the humans within them.

Deindustrialization and reindustrialization were indissoluble processes, propelled by productivity gains that led to an ever-greater proliferation of products.[17] In manufacturing, the 1975 workforce was identical in size to that in 2000, but the latter's output was double the 1975 output, a key factor in the expansion of the overall workforce from 94 million employees to 142.5 million during that quarter-century span.[18] The emphasis on deindustrialization by analysts of this phenomenon obscured the actual processes that caused this development.

With manufacturing as a stable base, the government, business, and service sectors continued to expand.[19] Any number of factors contributed to this: deficit spending by the government, credit system expansion by means of the financial sector, unrelenting pressure to cut wages and eliminate benefits, and an unfavorable balance of payments, whereby purchases of goods from outside the U.S. greatly outweighed sales to those same areas. But underlying it all was a manufacturing center that produced an ever-greater mass of commodities, a testament to its importance and centrality in the economy. Economic expansion in all areas rippled out from the center.

A century ago, throughout the last decades of the 1800s and into the first half of the 1900s, industrialization meant that all but a small sliver of the workforce was treated as expendable. Today's college graduates face an employment situation reminiscent of this era. Back then, in the agricultural sector, the family economy was supplemented by seasonal employees if and when growing conditions warranted. Within the factory system, longer-term business cycle fluctuations and the everyday vicissitudes of supply and demand produced similar types of employment insecurity. Small businesses and independent professionals were caught between these two spheres of economic activity and suffered alongside everyone else.

The prosperous decades following World War II appeared to reverse this pattern, only to be revealed as a relatively short-lived exception to the rules that have generally governed the market economy.

Employment reorganization

During the last decades of the twentieth century, economic reorganization took place on many levels: the globalization of trade and the reshuffling of economic blocs under the guise of free trade, a reorganized and innovative financial system that funneled speculative earnings towards a broad spectrum of the upper classes, and a productive mechanism so dispersed that it seemed to exist nowhere and everywhere all at once.[20]

97

As the economy began to expand outward and away from manufacturing, unions declined. From a peak of 21 million in 1979, union membership in the United States hovered around 14.8 million in 2015, nearly a third less and concentrated primarily in the public sector. Meantime, the labor force had expanded by more than half.[21] Several factors contributed to this trend. While the service sector had been resistant to unions, the unions had mostly ignored the service sector anyway.

Another factor—a more highly educated workforce—isn't usually associated with the decline of the unions. Nonetheless, for individuals, education became a means to guarantee a decent standard of living at a time when unions were less and less capable of doing the same. Higher education made union membership redundant. Daniel Hecker, known for his research on college-educated underemployment during the 1980s, wrote that "many high-wage jobs which required a high school diploma or less education disappeared, or were taken by those with more education."[22] Skilled machinists were replaced by computer operators.

While the high school-educated workforce disappeared and its college-educated complement expanded, wages followed accordingly. Recalculating wage rates to those prevailing in 2011, employees with less than a high school education experienced a decline in hourly wages from $15 to $12 since 1973. As a portion of the labor force, this group also dropped from 28.5 to 10.8 percent of all employees during that same time frame. High school graduates did not do much better.[23] While wage rates declined from $17 to $16 per hour, their share of the labor market shrank from 38.3 to 31.9 percent. Wages for employees with some college education virtually stagnated the entire time, even though their presence in the labor force grew by 10 percent. College graduates, on the other hand, did considerably better—from $25 per hour in 1973 to $28 in 2000, while their labor force presence nearly doubled from 10.1 to 18.8 percent.[24]

By 1970 already, the non-goods producing sectors (for example, service industries) accounted for 70 percent of the workforce (85 percent by 2009). Service sectors included finance, insurance, real estate, and banking; wholesale and retail trade; public utilities; transportation enterprises, and business, professional, and personal services.[25] Keep in mind, too, that while the service industries dwarf all other sectors, service occupations represent only 40 percent of the workforce. Within the banking sector, for instance, computer programmers and technicians focus on machines and functional systems, besides bank tellers and customer service staff who actually interact with clients and the public. Nonetheless, the workforce of the twenty-first century is a new entity, with the industrial proletariat overtaken by service-oriented personnel.[26]

Within the services sector, employees were split into two groups, with low-waged sales and service employment at one end and high-waged positions within the managerial, professional, and technical fields at the other. David Autor points out that there have been "expanding job opportunities in both high-skill, high wage occupations and low-skill, low-wage occupations." In general, "the decline in middle-skill jobs has been detrimental to the earnings and labor force participation rates of workers without a four-year college education, and differentially so for males, who are increasingly concentrated in low-paying service occupations."[27]

This same bifurcation occurred within individual firms. The skyrocketing of executive salaries is an often-told story. As explained by David Weil in *The Fissured Workplace* (2014), "the ratio between the pay received by the average CEO in total direct compensation and that of the average production worker went from 37.2:1 in 1979 to an astounding 277:1 in 2007."[28] Paul Osterman's *Securing Prosperity* (2001) noted still another workplace fissure, this one with special pertinence for employees with an advanced education:

> radical changes in the organization of work seem to be occurring in the midst of substantial internal dislocation and turmoil. That both are happening at the same time points to an apparent paradox: on the one hand some firms are broadening jobs and devolving higher levels of responsibility to their workforce, while on the other they are reducing their commitment to the same workforce and increasingly treating them as expendable.[29]

Public education was a casualty of the 1970s economic crisis. Declining educational standards accompanied and also fostered the low-wage service sector, with technological innovations serving as mediators and facilitators of those changes.[30] As numeracy declined, pictures replaced numbers on cash registers, change was computed digitally, and only basic counting remained as a necessary skill. Literacy skills also became less essential as word-processing programs came equipped with spelling and grammar checkers and automatic synonyms.

Today, texting has emerged as an evolving form of truncated language. On the managerial level, texting speeds communications by eliminating cumbersome conventions tied to phone and email interaction. Voice-to-text applications, in this case with machine-driven spelling and grammar protocols, have the potential to further simplify human involvement.

The division of the workworld into high- and low-wage sectors corresponded to levels of education. Employees with

Table 4.1 Occupation by levels of education, 1990[31]

Occupation	Professional degree	Master's degree	Baccalaureate degree	Associate degree	Vocational Certificate	Some college	High school
Managerial	4.9%	19.3%	20.0%	16.0%	8.2%	12.9%	8.0%
Professional	82.7	64.4	40.6	18.9	19.8	7.1	3.6
Technical	3.7	2.2	5.5	7.9	10.9	3.8	2.2
Sales/clerical/service	8.6	13.6	31.6	52.4	55.2	69.3	70.4
Mechanic/repairer/precision production/machine operator	0	0.5	1.3	3.1	4.5	4.2	11.3
Other	0	0	1.0	1.7	1.4	2.3	4.3

Compiled from: W. Norton Grubb, *Working in the Middle: Strengthening Education and Training for the Mid-Skilled Labor Force* (Jossey-Bass, 1996), p. 5.

graduate degrees, as seen in Table 4.1, were heavily clustered in the professional and managerial occupations, while those with only a high school or an associate degree were found in service areas. Already by 1990, baccalaureate degree holders were being pulled in the two contradictory directions, with two-thirds employed in managerial, professional, and technical occupations and the other third in areas focused on employees with less education.

Marginal employment, thought to be part of an older capitalism that was passing out of existence, made its reappearance in the late twentieth century in all sectors of the economy, including manufacturing, the service industries, and on the managerial and professional level.

These same workplace characteristics of part-time employment, short-term contracts, and "at will" workplace arrangements that provided neither benefits nor security were renamed the "gig economy" as the twenty-first century took shape. It was pitched to young college graduates and to employees in high-tech areas as worthy of adulation.

Underemployed college graduates, however, faced a mix of circumstances that combined features of both worlds—the marginal and the innovative. One college graduate explained that for the first time she was required to use a punch clock, even though she fielded questions from medical doctors about drug regimens for a large pharmaceutical company. Paid by the hour, and with no benefits of any kind, employees accumulated "points" for rules infractions such as returning from lunch a few minutes late. Four "points" could result in dismissal. David Weil describes these types of work situations:

The modern workplace has been profoundly transformed. Employment is no longer the clear relationship between a well-defined employer and a worker. The basic terms of employment—hiring, evaluation, pay, supervision, training, coordination—are now the result of multiple organizations.

These traits were especially evident in the low-waged service sector, where "small businesses tend to have a higher proportion of their costs related to labor."[32]

Job turnover rates increased for people caught in these new dynamics.[33] Working hours also increased, such that "the average American actually worked 199 hours more in 2000 than in 1973, a period of three decades during which worker productivity per hour nearly doubled."[34] This equaled an additional five weeks per year. Except for the elite, dual-earner households became a necessity in terms of upward mobility or even maintaining a stable standard of living during an era in which individuals faced stagnant wages.[35]

Young people were deeply affected by these changes, but so was everyone who had children. Arne Kalleberg explains: "the fact that nearly every available adult in the United States is now in paid employment (or looking for paid work) has had a profound effect on the ability of families to meet the personal needs of working adults or to care for children, the sick, and the elderly."[36] The husband as the sole-breadwinner, for instance, has fallen to below 18 percent of heterosexual married-couple families.[37]

Examining the data in Table 4.2, we can see significant shifts in the distribution of occupations. The new capitalism looked very different.

Each category warrants close scrutiny. The near-total eclipse of the farming community has been mentioned previously. Agriculture today in the United States is almost exclusively a corporate matter. Business proprietors, as part of the managerial-professional group, are similarly marginalized, constituting only 2.7 percent occupationally.

Table 4.2   Distribution of occupations 1870, 1940, and 2009 (percent)

Occupation	1870	1940	2009
Farmers and farm laborers	46.0	17.3	1.1
Blue-collar occupations (craft workers, operatives, laborers)	33.5	38.7	19.9
Service occupations (clerical, sales, domestic service, other)	12.6	28.1	41.4
Managers, professionals, and proprietors	8.0	15.1	37.6

Source: Robert J. Gordon, *The Rise and Fall of American Growth: The U.S. Standard of Living Since the Civil War* (Princeton University Press, 2016), p. 53.

Blue-collar occupations have gone through several phases. In the first, between 1870 and 1940, there was a shift from craft workers to operatives with the rise of the factory system, a change that replaced skilled labor with semi-skilled. Since then, all forms of blue-collar work have declined. The low-level service occupations, on the other hand, have flourished. A huge expansion also categorizes managers, officials, and professionals—that is, the college-educated workforce.

* * *

If a relative deindustrialization took place in the twentieth century, masking an actual reindustrialization, an *absolute* deindustrialization, with a drastic reduction of the manufacturing workforce, is a product of the twenty-first century. The loss of jobs is overwhelming, even though it has occurred without the intense scrutiny of previous decades. From 17.3 million employees in mid-2000, manufacturing employment dipped to

11.5 million by the beginning of 2010, before rebounding a bit in the next years (to 12.7 million in August 2018).[38]

The ongoing focus of commentators on neoliberalism, taken to be a retreat from government intervention into economic affairs and a return to market-based mechanisms, has thus missed some of the crucial processes that have been at work during this entire last half-century.[39] Government spending has become more important than ever. As a percent of gross domestic product, debt on the federal level alone is now three times as great as it was in 1970. It equals in value the annual production of all goods and services nationwide.[40]

How the government spends money, however, has changed. Rather than funding subsidies intended for the lower classes, direct grants for corporate entities have taken precedence, principally through military spending. The government is unable to reduce overall expenditures without sluggish growth and recessionary conditions as a result. In the words of Paul Mattick:

> the world economy had moved from the self-regulating mechanism imagined by free-market enthusiasts towards a system dependent on constant management by governmental authorities—and one in which the relaxation of management, or the limitations on its reach, would make way for dire developments.[41]

Nor has it mattered which political party is in power. While the Republicans are known for cutting government budgets on the local and state levels, federal debt tends to expand more quickly when they control the Presidency. Insofar as the Democrats follow a set pattern, it tends towards the opposite direction.[42]

Deindustrialization generally benefitted women, another point overlooked in the literature. Workforce participation rates and wages rose for them, while men headed in the opposite direction. Women also outpaced men educationally. Deindustrialization helped break down entrenched systems of racial, ethnic, and gender exclusion. That it took a thorough-going reorganization of the economy to bring about some measure of advance for women and minorities gives an indication of how deeply embedded these prejudices are.

Ultimately, though, there were no true winners, except at the top of the social ladder. Wages, benefits, and employment conditions have either deteriorated or stagnated for every section of the working population since the 1970s, even though women's relative position improved dramatically. The working class has become the working poor.

Despite the huge overall reductions in wages and benefits that now typify many workplaces, the economy continues to function at a sluggish rate of growth. The technological revolution of the past decades has transformed many aspects of social life, but it has also proven unable to enliven the economy in any deep-seated manner. This is the world into which college students are catapulted.

The college premium conundrum

The rise in college-educated underemployment first caught people's attention in the early 1970s. In retrospect, the bump of an additional 3 percentage points, from 10.8 percent in 1967 to 13.8 percent in 1975, appears relatively minor, but at the time it provoked widespread consternation about the falling value of a college degree.[43] Discussions focused on the "college premium"—that is, the difference in earnings between a four-year college degree and a high school diploma. During the 1970s, the gap between college graduates and high school graduates narrowed. Perhaps a college degree wasn't all that it had been cracked up to be during the previous decades?

Beginning in the 1980s, though, wages for baccalaureate recipients began to escalate. From then on, the trend has been for the college premium to widen. Its increase now led observers to conclude that college graduates were under-supplied, rather than oversupplied, as had been the case only recently. How else to explain the increase in wages? More college graduates were apparently needed to satisfy employer demand.[44] Significant gaps in income existed in terms of educational levels achieved.

Yet, this was precisely the same period of time when underemployment was rising. Pegged around 10 percent in 1967, estimates had doubled or even tripled in some calculations to 20–30 percent of college graduates by 1990.[45] Something did not make sense. How could both be true at once, a state of affairs that seemed to defy economic logic? Either a good is under-supplied (hence, the rising college premium) or it is over-supplied (the rise in underemployment). In the case of college graduates, nonetheless, this was the situation that prevailed: underemployment and simultaneously a widening gap between the graduates of four-year colleges and everyone else with less education.

Several explanations have been offered to account for this conundrum, which taken together tell us much about the evolution of the economy. For one, the gap in earnings between college and high school graduates did not necessarily widen because college graduates have done so well, but instead, because others (for example, high school graduates) have done so much worse. This partly accounts for the earning trends of the last several decades. Those with higher levels of education have descended more slowly than their lesser-educated peers.

Downward mobility became a matter of relative disadvantage.[46] The gap between college graduates and non-college graduates widened as everyone raced towards the bottom, but at different rates of acceleration.

John Marsh, author of *Class Dismissed: Why We Cannot Teach Or Learn Our Way Out of Inequality* (2011), offers two complementary explanations. First, as just explained, "the average college graduate ... has gotten wealthier relative to the average high school graduate, mostly because the wages of high school graduates have dropped." But he hastens to add that "the equally important story about inequality is that it is the truly blessed (or clever or calculating) college graduate who has gotten wealthier compared to everyone else, including other college graduates."[47]

Richard Vedder adds further clarification to help decipher the college premium conundrum: "at the top of the earnings and income distribution, large growth was observed from 1990 to 2009, a growth that raised average earnings for all college graduates a good bit, counteracting a likely decline in the status of the bottom one-third or so of college earners."[48] Among that "bottom third or so of college earners" are many of the underemployed graduates.

Thus, a new dividing line has emerged, a bifurcation of the college-educated into two distinct groups. At the upper end tend to be graduates in cutting-edge fields like computer science, finance, and economics, in which salaries can be quite high and rates of underemployment relatively low (for example, only 30–40 percent for recent graduates!). At the other end of the spectrum, with low starting salaries and high rates of underemployment (for example, over 50 percent) are pre-professional fields like leisure and hospitality or public policy and law. But also, many areas within the liberal arts fit this pattern as well, such as anthropology, biology, and psychology. Advanced mathematical ability has become a fault line, replacing the diplomas (high school and college) that came before it. This also explains the anomalous drop-outs—few in number despite the extensive press—whose talents positioned them to earn great wealth.

Finally, there is the ever-elusive Say's Law, named after the French economist, Jean-Baptiste Say, who in 1803 suggested that "supply creates its own demand," or in this case as per Vedder, "the supply of diplomas created the demand for them." Anthony Carnevale explains: "businesses pay more money to workers with degrees than to those without because employers believe that postsecondary educated workers are more valuable."[49]

Differences even emerge within specific occupational categories. "First-line supervisors of retail sales workers" with a high school diploma have median earnings of $35,500; in comparison, their college graduate colleagues earn $50,000. Among "general office clerks," employees with a high school diploma have median earnings of $32,500; for a bachelor's degree recipient, it is $37,100.[50] For male "laborers and freight, stock, and material movers" with some college or an associate's degree, average annual earnings are $21,000; with a bachelor's degree, you earn $25,000. For female "teaching assistants," the difference per year is $700: $15,500 versus $16,200.[51]

For college graduates, though, a second wave of deindustrialization seems to be pending.[52] High-level service positions have been vulnerable in each of the economic downturns ever since the 1990s. Whether this will become a generalized phenomenon remains to be seen, but the indications so far give no grounds for optimism. This matter we turn to in the next chapter.

5

Class status and economic instability

Uncertainty is part of the new precarity. For college graduates, it may be the only aspect of life that is guaranteed. It is not just economic laws that determine their future, but political interventions and social reactions also contribute to an unbalanced and ever-changing situation. These graduates must make decisions about their futures at a time when there is a growing consensus that their fate has less and less to do with individual choice. The border between elusion and illusion has been blurred.

Underemployed college graduates are the latest addition to a working class under intense pressure. The bottom levels of society are caught in a deep tumult where people cycle in-and-out of poverty. Over a two-year period, an entire third of the nation's population—more than 100 million people—falls below the official poverty threshold. One-fifth of the population remains there for six months or more, one-seventh—some 40 million people—are mired there for at least a year.[1] The fact that poverty touches so many people gets lost in the everyday assumption of a stable, quasi-permanent class of the downtrodden. That isn't at all what modern-day poverty looks like.

Behind those figures lies an even grimmer reality. Poverty-level thresholds are set artificially low, lest government benefit programs become alternatives to the wages offered by employers.[2] The last major readjustment of public support programs occurred during the mid-1990s, an overhaul considered long overdue.

Previous retrofits of these policies occurred every few decades. During the 1930s, widespread unemployment, under-employment, and poverty prompted the creation of a federally funded system. The New Deal supplanted the overwhelmed and inadequate systems that were either privately endowed, often by religious associations and charities, or financed by local and state tax bases. A second major overhaul, the War on Poverty, occurred during the 1960s, as a response to the Civil Rights Movement and the migration of southern blacks into the crowded, unhealthy ghettoes of the North, Midwest, and West.

The economic boom of the 1990s reversed this pattern. Government relief programs were curtailed so that they would not dissuade potential workers from filling the low-wage needs of the service sector. Policymakers were convinced that a tightening, rather than an expansion, of welfare rules was due and that a government-funded safety net was needed less than ever. The newfound affluence of that decade had lulled the political and business elites into thinking that prosperous times were here to stay.

The Personal Responsibility and Work Opportunity Reconciliation Act of 1996 became one of the signature accomplishments of the Clinton administration, so successful that welfare largely disappeared as a contentious political issue. Welfare recipients were forced to work as a condition of receiving benefits, thus removing any temptation to substitute government support for employment characterized by low quality and miserly compensation.

With or without these alterations, however, official poverty rates have hovered at 10–15 percent of the population ever since the mid-1960s. A fourth of those living in poverty are children; another 15 percent are over the age of 65.[3] This is to say that nearly half of those in poverty are either not yet able or no longer capable of working for a living.

Poverty thresholds are measured in terms of basic and near-basic existence. In 2016, a mother and child had to subsist on an income below $16,895 to qualify.[4] Poverty levels are also used to measure the degree of need and are often adjusted to fit actual circumstances, such as 200 percent of poverty, used by some government agencies and private charities to certify possible recipients.

Constant turmoil takes a heavy toll. For the poor, instability is a feature of everyday life. Nearly everyone (86 percent) in the lowest quintile of the population experiences a change in income of greater than 25 percent from one year to the next, split almost evenly between those who see an increase and those whose fortunes decline even further.[5] For a single mother with one dependent earning $15,000 (30 hours per week at $10 per hour), an additional $3,750 represents a 25 percent boost that moves her above the poverty line. Rags-to-riches folklore, in terms of sudden leaps upward, takes on pertinent meaning in this situation.

This is why, too, a minimal redistribution of income from the top to the bottom would have little impact at the high end but would represent a substantial, even if insufficient, improvement at the low end. Income within the top quintile in 2017 averaged $221,846. For them, a change of $3,750 would barely be noticeable.[6]

Larry Summers, formerly U.S. Treasury Secretary and ex-president of Harvard University, estimated that simply freezing income distribution rates at their 1979 levels would be enough to give each family in the bottom 80 percent of the population an additional $11,000, but would cost the top 1 percent only $750,000.[7] Measured over the 35-year period used in Summers's calculation, this would have amounted to $21,500 per year for people who already had an average after-tax income of $286,300 in 1979 and $862,700 in 2000.[8]

Summers isn't actually suggesting that this be done, since anything that remotely hints of expropriation is considered off-limits by all sectors of the political world. If anything, the trend over the past half-century has been to award a larger portion of the social product to the wealthy.

Poverty, however, does not mean material deprivation in a literal sense. In another indication of the vast outpouring of commodities from the factory system, the poor are often surrounded by material possessions. More than 90 percent of poor households have televisions, phones, refrigerators, and microwaves; more than 80 percent live with air conditioning, while three-quarters have a car, truck, or van, and more than half own a washer and dryer.[9]

Often missing is the right mix of commodities to maintain a minimally decent standard of living. For this, sufficient income is needed, precisely what the poor lack. Poverty reduces access to services, and in the modern economy, this is a critical variable. Even though labor has grown cheaper in comparison to capital (hence, the increases in production and productivity), personal services are still costly. Replacing a home's hot water heater, for instance, can cost as much in labor charges as it does for the appliance itself.

The working poor

The notion that welfare is aimed at the work-shy is out of touch with today's reality. In the aftermath of the 2007–08 Great

Recession, a full 25 percent of the nation's employees lived in households that qualified for supplemental income or benefits from the government; in other words, "nearly three-quarters (73 percent) of enrollments in America's major public benefits programs are from working families."[10]

What kinds of establishments characterize the low-wage sector? More than one might think—all aspects of the retail trade, many services, small companies, and businesses with high employee turnover.[11] Small companies with fewer than twenty employees account for nearly one in five jobs overall, a segment of the economy traditionally characterized by the sub-baccalaureate labor market.[12]

A wage of $15 per hour, or $31,200 per year for full-time employees (before taxes and other deductions) has emerged as the standard for a living wage and threshold for a minimum existence, yet "forty-two (42) percent of U.S. workers make less than $15 per hour." Nearly half of them are over the age of 35. Low-wage employment is pervasive in every place where the public comes into contact with business: the food industry, retail shops, personal care services, clinical and hospital healthcare services, janitorial services, transportation, customer service representatives, receptionists, and more.[13] If an employee receives tips, it is a tell-tale sign that their overall compensation is inadequate.[14] Well-paid employees don't need tips.

Of all the governmental funds spent on public assistance programs, both on state and federal levels, most goes to working families.[15] In fact, every major area of the economy employs massive numbers of workers—many of them full-time—who subsidize their paltry wages with government benefits: "the families of more than half of the fast-food workers employed 40 or more hours per week", for instance, "are enrolled in public assistance programs." In manufacturing, a third of the families of full-time production workers receive some sort of government support.[16] In banking, a similar percentage of the half-million bank tellers (one-third) qualifies for subsidies.[17] Of home care workers, 48 percent receive public assistance; in child care, it is 46 percent. Among part-time college faculty, some one-quarter receive food, health, or income subsidies from the government.[18] Even the government must subsidize 15 percent of its own employees (listed under Public Administration in Figure 5.1), given the fractured nature of governance on the federal, state, and local levels.

Without the government, the market mechanism as it relates to the huge low-wage sectors of the economy would

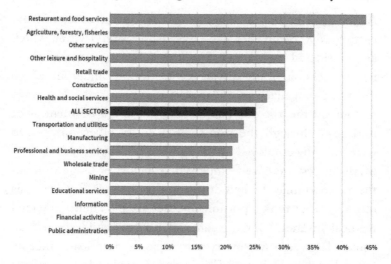

Figure 5.1 Share of workers with family member enrolled in public programs by industry[19]

Source: Sylvia A. Allegretto, Marc Doussard, Dave Graham-Squire, Ken Jacobs, Dan Thompson, and Jeremy Thompson, "Fast Food, Poverty Wages: The Public Cost of Low-Wage Jobs in the Fast-Food Industry," http://laborcenter.berkeley.edu, October 2013, pp. 1, 7. Reprinted with permission: UC Berkeley Center for Labor Research and Education.

break down. Government support provides a hefty subsidy to low-wage employers. The contemporary discourse on "neo-liberalism" misses the true significance of this development. Government is more subservient to business needs than ever before, and the business-government symbiosis constitutes a last link on which continued economic functioning hinges. Just as we saw with the for-profit educational sector, the entire service sector would deteriorate dramatically without this level of government intervention.

The gig economy

At the other end of the employment and income spectrum are cutting-edge companies like Uber, Apple, and Twitter, which are considered the vanguard of the new economy. Yet these newer, technologically driven companies are underpinned by the same casualization of labor that supports the low-wage sectors. Of the 160,000 people who found employment as of mid-2015 through the ride-sharing entity Uber, only 4,000 were formally employed by the company.

All the rest were "self-employed." One driver bragged about the 140,000 miles he had driven in the last year. But from his revenue, Uber took a portion, another sizable chunk provided medical insurance for himself and his two children, and an equally large sum was reserved to repay an auto loan, since he figured a new vehicle would be needed annually. Media accounts peg average compensation at places like Uber at the living wage threshold of $15 per hour.[20] At Fed Ex, where average wages are much higher, delivery drivers nonetheless must own their own trucks. They too are treated as independent contractors, with all the attendant liabilities that such a designation entails.[21]

Apple claims that it "is one of the biggest job creators in the United States, responsible for two million jobs in all 50 states." Only 4 percent of those two million, however, receive paychecks from Apple itself. Another 450,000 are employed by Apple's 9,000 supplier companies. The remaining 1.5 million jobs are "U.S. jobs attributable to the App Store ecosystem," whatever that is.[22] According to one online job site, a "specialist" with high-level technical and communication skills who functions as a retail salesperson at an Apple Store can expect wages that range between $10–$22 per hour and average $15.04, right at the cusp of a living wage.[23]

To be sure, there are often technical grounds for outsourcing work to supplier firms. If only a few precision machinists are needed, for instance, it makes sense for a company to contract with a firm that has a wider array of personnel, skill levels, and equipment, rather than attempting to piece together the exact combination of employees, machines, and materials that this would take.

But this is only one motivation for outsourcing. Cheaper labor in the form of lower wages, and an absence of benefits and regulations pertaining to the workplace and the environment, are the most common critical factors these days. Companies like Apple do not make these distinctions in their publicity materials, even though cost is a primary consideration in their decision making. The economic altruism that Apple projects is built on a foundation of substandard wages and less than satisfactory working conditions, both within the United States and even more so on an international level.

A company like Twitter, despite its outsized media presence, had only 3,860 employees in total when it announced plans to cut its staff in late 2016.[24] With so few employees, it has virtually no impact on the job market despite its importance for everyday social discourse.

Keep in mind too that employment figures change alongside the business fortunes of these very same companies, thus contributing to the precarious nature of employment. A sudden fall from profitability, as with Twitter, can eliminate thousands of jobs. But regardless of whether we examine these companies' tumultuous business paths or the relentless subjugation of their workforces to outsourcing and casualization, the future of employment looks grim indeed.

Employment in the new economy is, in any case, a mirage. The much-touted "gig" economy encompasses "nonemployer firms" that gross, by definition, at least $1,000 per year. In popular parlance, these are individual contractors and freelancers. Even though there are almost 25 million such "businesses" in the United States, they only account for some 3 percent of total business receipts. The overwhelming majority of "nonemployer firms" do not yield enough revenue to support a single person; 16 million of them generate gross revenues of less than $25,000 per year, another 3.5 million less than $50,000 per year, out of which expenses and supplies must be deducted.[25]

Many of these "nonemployer firms" appear to be "second" jobs that supplement earnings from elsewhere and are only relied on in exigent circumstances. They offer flexible hours, but at unreliable rates of pay and without benefits. Yet, in one survey, two-thirds of the respondents claimed that their business constituted their primary source of income.[26] Self-employment becomes still another definition used to disguise the downtrodden. If all the self-employed are considered (not just the "nonemployer firms"), along with their employees, we gain still another measure of smallness. These businesses account for 30 percent of all jobs nationwide.[27]

The number of "nonemployer firms" dwarfs the number of businesses with employees, of which there are only 5.7 million in the United States. Small firms are responsible for small amounts of business, and most "employer firms" are quite small. Sixty percent have four or fewer employees and account in total for less than 1 percent of all business receipts and 5 percent of employees. Almost 90 percent of all firms have fewer than twenty employees and generate just over 12 percent of all employer-firm business receipts.[28]

To flip this measure on its head, 10 percent of firms account for 88 percent of all business, a ratio that mirrors in its own peculiar way the concentration of income and wealth by the elite. At the very top are the ten largest technology firms, which alone account for 5.5 percent of the nation's gross domestic product.[29] Another way to view this is that relatively few employees account for an outsized amount of overall business activity.

Higher education and diversity

Throughout the last decades of the twentieth century and up to the present, college enrollments outstripped population growth by a 2–1 margin. Between 2000 and 2010, however, an additional 5.7 million students were added at a pace that more than tripled population growth and more than quadrupled the growth of the labor force. Except for occasional dips, perpetual expansion has characterized the entire history of higher education.[30]

Rapid growth has allowed the collegiate system to achieve many of its goals. These include the upscaling of educational credentials throughout all levels of society. It has also incorporated historically underrepresented minorities, especially blacks, latinx, and new immigrants, into the collegiate system in unprecedented numbers. Expansion has meant that all demographic groups could be accommodated, even if at different rates. The competitive pressures that help propel racial and ethnic antagonisms, as a consequence, were eased over a period of many decades.

Since 1976, when data collection about such matters began, the enrollment of black students increased from 9.6 percent of the undergraduate population nationwide to a high point of 15.2 percent in 2011. This represents a three-fold increase in the number of black students. Enrollments for Hispanics have been even more dramatic, a nine-fold gain in the number of students, from 3.6 to 18.2 percent of the total undergraduate student body by 2016.

The population of white students also grew, in this case by nearly 3 million by 2010. But whereas whites represented 84.3 percent of the student body in 1976, by 2016 they were just 56.9 percent.[31] There were more white students in absolute terms, but they represented a declining proportion of college students overall.

The legal and legislative challenges to affirmative action in education have largely focused on the admissions practices at elite publicly financed institutions where enrollments are limited.[32] Law and medical schools have been a primary target because of their tight rein on the number of new students, whereas graduate programs in, say, public administration and business, two areas that have briskly expanded enrollments, have been untouched by these sorts of outside pressures.[33] In these instances, social class underlies issues of race and access.

Entire state systems of higher education have also been subject to court-sanctioned challenges, but the principal target in these cases has been the flagship institutions. Other state-sponsored schools are not nearly as selective and not nearly as much in contention. A third area of legal and legislative conflict has been race-designated scholarship and fellowship programs, again revealing the financial underpinnings that motivate challenges to anything that upsets preexisting patterns of preferences (such as legacy admissions and priority for athletes).

Growth, then, has not eliminated racial and ethnic tensions, but it has narrowed the scope of activity for discriminatory practices and outright bigotry. As the economy slows, however, so too does the expansionary aspects of higher education. Overall enrollments have slipped. So have enrollments for blacks since their peak in 2011. Enrollments for whites have also begun to decline. A narrowing of access may be one of the outcomes of any longer-term constriction of the educational system, not necessarily because of a rekindling of prejudice but because economic difficulties find some measure of resolution within educational institutions.

Meantime, many areas of graduate education have remained overwhelmingly white, despite attempts over the last fifty years to diversify the student body. Blacks comprise only 6.3 percent of the students at medical schools across the country, latinx only 6.9 percent, individuals of multiple race background, 2.7 percent. Medical schools are functioning at a level of diversity that undergraduate education surpassed four decades ago.[34]

Faculty have diversified at a much slower rate than their students. Just over one-fifth of all faculty belong to a minority group. Full professors are the most homogenous group, representing a demographic that belongs to the past.[35]

Even though the number of full-time faculty has doubled since 1970, they have shrunk as a proportion of total faculty, from three-fourths to only half.[36] Because enrollment growth has been used to counter declining rates of government support and increased costs for student recruitment and retention, inexpensive adjuncts, paid by the course and mostly without benefits, have become an alternative. Half the professoriate is thus part of the downtrodden contingent workforce.

The relative decline in the number of full-time faculty, however, coincided with positive developments in terms of diversity. Just as deindustrialization brought with it positive openings for women, so too the decline of full-time faculty has opened the professoriate to new levels of integration. This is an oft repeated pattern, in which genuine improvements for some come at the expense of the previous, albeit exclusive, beneficiaries. Equality takes on peculiar meanings in a society in which resources are kept scarce.

If higher education has diversified racially and ethnically, both for students and for faculty, this has not been true socioeconomically. The diversification of higher education has paralleled the stratification of the population rather than undermined it.

Goldie Blumenstyk points out that "wealthier people have always been better educated than low-income people." But between 1970 and 2012, she tells us:

> the proportion of low-income twenty-four-year-olds (family income of $34,160 and below) with bachelor's degrees went from just 6 percent to slightly over 8 percent. Meanwhile, the proportion of upper income twenty-four-year-olds (family income of $108,650 and up) with a bachelor's degree increased from 40 percent to 73 percent.[37]

The expansion of the higher education system has mostly taken place at the upper ends of the income tier. To reiterate:

"it is clear that with growing economic inequality and slowing economic growth the effects of family background on one's ultimate economic success are more important than they used to be."[38]

The elite

Like the population in general, the elite exists within a hierarchy where boundaries are often indistinct. For our purposes, though, we can distinguish two main groups. The larger of them includes the upper middle class and now comprises some 18–22 percent of the population.[39] It is proportionally bigger than ever before as a result of the funneling of resources towards the upper strata of society during the last half-century.

Many members of this group remain intimately involved in the circumstances of their own success—that is, they are not so wealthy that they can live by means of wealth alone. Doctors, lawyers, the owners of medium-sized businesses, mid-level administrators in the corporate world, and upper-level administrators in the government and nonprofit sectors belong to this segment of the population, as do their dependents.

At the very top and constituting its own self-contained world, resides the second group, which for our purposes can be referred to as the "real bourgeoisie." Sometimes identified as the top 5 or 10 percent, more precise analyses confine it to within the upper 1 percent of society, sometimes as little as the upper 1/100th of 1 percent. What characterizes this group is its enormous wealth, so great that the need to work is obviated. Members of this group are beholden to no one, a trait true for them alone, even though economic vicissitudes often affect the magnitude of their fortunes.

While this group includes the "idle rich"—people who live off inherited wealth, often accumulated by a forefather a half-century or more ago—most of its members belong to the top echelons of the business world, with others scattered throughout government, the arts, nonprofit foundations, sports and entertainment, and elsewhere in society. These are the people who negotiate the decisions that determine the fate that befalls everyone else.

The upper classes have benefitted financially by doing nothing at all. Not hard work (even though many work hard), but the appreciation in value of real estate, stocks, bonds, and other financial instruments accounts for their great success in the last decades. Hefty salary increases that applied to them alone have also helped.

While nearly everyone else was restricted by the wage and salary parameters of their occupations, the wealthy had investments in areas removed from structural constraints. Insofar as the idea of "neoliberal" has meaning, this is where it does. How else to explain why the wealthy did so well during an era when everyone else treaded water or worked harder just to stay in place?

Except for the bourgeoisie, wealth exists in a form where assets remain inconvertible, as with pension funds and housing. Pensions alone account for a third of all household wealth.[40] And for the population as a whole, homeownership has remained stable in the 60–65 percent range ever since the early 1960s. The sole exception was the few years prior to the 2007–08 Great Recession, when homeownership rates increased by nearly 5 percent, only to revert to the historic norm because of the mortgage crisis.[41]

In terms of wealth, a huge gap separates the upper 20 percent of the population from everyone else, illustrated in Table 5.1:[42]

Table 5.1 Wealth and income, by population quintile

Population	Share of wealth	Average net worth	Share of money income
81–100%	88.9%	$2,061,600	51.5%
61–80%	9.4%	$216,900	22.9%
41–60%	2.6%	$61,000	14.2%
21–40%	0.2%	$5,500	8.3%
Bottom 20%	-1.2%	$-27,500	3.1%

Compiled from: Lawrence Mishel, Josh Bivens, Elise Gould, and Heidi Shierholz, *The State of Working America*, twelfth edition (Cornell University Press, 2012), pp. 380–381, 387, for 2010 Wealth and Net Worth; U.S. Census Bureau, "Income and Poverty in the United States: 2016,", Table 2, for 2016 Money Income.

The bottom 20 percent of the population has debts greater than assets. The bottom 40 percent could not exist more than a few months without some sort of new income, even if they sold everything they possess. The bottom 80 percent taken as a whole owns only 3.5 percent of all stocks (8.3 percent if retirement accounts are included) and 29.9 percent of total housing equity. Despite the considerable attention devoted to the stock market by the media, it is information relevant only to the upper sliver of society.

Viewed historically, the pattern is even worse. A third of families owned less wealth in 2013 than they had in 1983. The middle half of families experienced no change at all. The top 20 percent, however, saw their median net wealth more than double.[43]

When we speak about inherited wealth, monetary gifts, and other modes of wealth transfer, we are addressing an issue that pertains almost exclusively to the top one-fifth of families. About half of all transfers between 1989 and 2010 were for less than $100,000. The average amount, though, was $448,400, a large sum but more of a supplement to other income streams than a substitute for them. The top 1 percent of families, on the other hand, accounted for one-third of all wealth transfers. As Edward Wolff, perhaps the foremost authority on this topic, explains, "the inequality of wealth transfers among recipients is about the same as that of household net worth."[44] When it comes to inherited wealth, then, death mirrors life.

Upper middle-class dominance of the educational system overlaps with its possession of wealth. A new type of "inter-generational wage" has emerged, as parents invest in their children's immediate well-being. Income and wealth are increasingly used to cushion the downward mobility of the children. "Young adults with parents in the top quartile of the income distribution," reported one set of researchers, "received six times the amount of financial assistance as young adults whose parents were in the bottom quartile."[45] Student loans, still thought to be the responsibility of graduates, are slowly shifting back towards their parents.

This type of parental sharing of wealth seems to have become more generalized with the spread of underemployment among college graduates. No longer confined to key lifecycle moments like marriage, starter homes, and childbirth, parental support becomes a key factor, for example, for anyone who pursues a creative endeavor as anything other than a hobby. For many artists, musicians, writers, and actors, the vast majority of whom are unable—despite their talents—to earn a steady or sufficient income, outside support is essential.

In the absence of government funding for the arts, wealthy benefactors take its place—in this case, well-to-do parents. The wealth and income gap between the elite and everyone else helps support the arts by means of familial subsidies for their children. The production of culture remains quite restricted class-wise, even though its dissemination has become universal.

* * *

While the population grew 17 percent between 1997 and 2014, the number of households with assets greater than $5 million (not including primary residences) multiplied by a factor greater than 4.5.[46] Median household income that last year for the entire population equaled $53,718. For the chief executives at the 500 largest U.S. companies in 2012, average compensation equaled $3.508 million per CEO. With stock options, bonuses, and other perks, remuneration totaled $10.5 million for each.[47]

It is the enormity of the wealth at the top of society that attracts the most attention. Cast the net a bit wider and we find that "the wealthiest 100 members of the *Forbes* list alone own about as much wealth as the entire African American population of 42 million." Even more, "America's 20 wealthiest people—a group that could fit comfortably in one single Gulfstream G650 luxury jet—now own more wealth than the bottom half of the American population combined, a total of 152 million people in 57 million households."[48]

With so much income and wealth accruing to the upper orders, the gap between them and everyone else has deepened significantly.

By defining middle-income as the range between two-thirds of median income on the low side and double that of median income on the high side (in this set of calculations, between $42,000 to $126,000 annually for a household of three), analysts at the Pew Research Center documented the push towards the lower and upper tiers of society. Between 1971 and 2015, the low-income sector increased from 25 to 29 percent of the population, the middle-income group declined from 61 to

50 percent, and the upper-income households expanded from 14 to 21 percent.[49]

There is one further measure that we can use to gauge the nature of contemporary society. The tumultuous precarity that characterizes the bottom rungs of society, with a third of the population circling in and out of poverty over a two-year period, is paralleled by similar tumult within the upper rungs. At some point in their lives, 70 percent of the population will have spent at least a year among the top 20 percent of all income-earners. Slightly more than one out of ten will spend a year or more among the top 1 percent.[50]

Few remain there, but again we see that the rags-to-riches tale isn't all mythology. Not the stratification of the population into discrete income ranks, but the constant churning of people into and out of wealth and poverty is what characterizes contemporary society. Instability is omnipresent, even though its impact is skewed by means of the stratification process.

6

Into the future

All of social life has been transformed by the economic alterations of the last half-century. Some changes are specific to the world of education, others are diffused throughout society. Multi-generation households are on the rise, for example, with almost double the proportion of young adults now living with their parents than was the case in 1970.[1] Independent living is no longer assumed as a next step after graduation. Even the likelihood of marriage correlates with educational attainment. While the general trend towards marriage declined to only half of all adults during the half-century between 1960 and 2013, among recipients of a bachelor's degree, the rate is 63 percent, for those with a high school diploma, 45 percent.[2]

Also important is the rise in racial diversity nationally, to which college graduates are distinct contributors. It is in this realm that a key goal of the higher education community has been realized. The collegiate environment has become increasingly diverse, a characteristic that parallels the general social trend. The population without baccalaureate degrees, for example, is "more racially diverse than it was three decades ago, with more than one-third comprising African Americans (13 percent), Latinos (20 percent), and Asian Americans (4 percent)." The college population mirrors this diversity: whites constitute slightly more than half of all students (56.7 percent), blacks 13.7 percent, latinx 15.2 percent, Asian Americans 6.9 percent.[3]

Residential patterns have followed this same trajectory, reversing some of the segregation that characterized previous times.[4] The gentrification of lower-income urban neighborhoods likewise has an educational component, although two distinct phenomena tend to get lumped together. Ever since the 1970s, college students and recent graduates have moved to low-income minority and immigrant neighborhoods because they offered cheaper rents and access to public transportation systems. This type of influx did not radically destabilize preexisting neighborhoods, if only because the students rented rather than purchased apartments and other living spaces. They too shared the crowded living conditions that typified these urban areas.

A separate phenomenon involves college graduates exclusively, often in the form of young professionals. This is where parental wealth plays a role in the form of down payments on apartments and houses. The young professionals attract real estate developers and speculators, with neither group hesitating to evict and deplete entire neighborhoods of their traditional inhabitants.[5] These transformed communities cater to different types of small businesses—cafes and restaurants for instance, whereas many of the preexisting retail establishments—like hardware stores, or newspaper and cigarette stands, and small grocery shops and bodegas, can no longer afford the new rent structures.

This helps explain still another demographic change. While racial and ethnic integration has moved forward (although gentrification then reverses this pattern), income segregation has intensified. More of the poor are clustered in poor neighborhoods, and more of the wealthy in rich ones. Meantime, the middle is shrinking.[6] In metropolitan regions with populations greater than 500,000, as seen in Figure 6.1, this has been true ever since 1970.

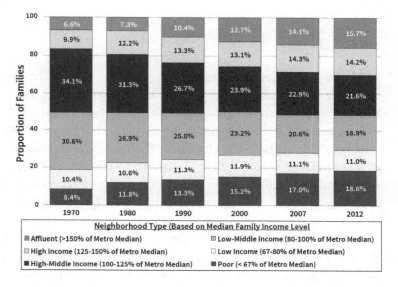

Figure 6.1 Proportion of families living in high-, middle-, and low-income neighborhoods

Source: Sean F. Reardon and Kendra Bischoff, "The Continuing Increase in Income Segregation, 2007–2012," https://cepa.stanford.edu, March 2016, pp. 6–7, 17. Reprinted with permission: Stanford Center for Education Policy Analysis.

The income-segregated neighborhoods mirror the class-based patterns that have strengthened within society and within the collegiate system at large, whereby one's parents have a powerful bearing not only on the present but on the future as well.

The educated underclass, already foreclosed from occupations that match their degrees, find fewer affordable housing options available to them. They are hardly alone in this plight. To rent living quarters is a misfortune that demands large portions of your income in return for space that is often too small, awkwardly constructed, and unattractive in many essentials.[7]

Mobility forestalled

A liberal-arts college education was once thought to be a guarantee of a middle-class existence. That belief is now gone, both because education no longer means what it did previously and because the middle is disappearing. Today's college graduates are caught in the crosshairs of economic dislocation. A new division has emerged, not measured by education but by employment. Specifically, the new dividing line presupposes a college education, but it also divides the graduates in terms of employment commensurate with that education.

The modern middle class was dependent for its creation on the expansion of government services as an economic sector and on government funding to prop up the business world. Government agencies guaranteed decent wages and steady employment to their own personnel, and this had an elevating effect on the competitive sector in terms of its treatment of the workforce. This was the high point of the post-World War II era. A significant gap still separates public from private employment. For the 22 million government employees, average annual wages are $56,870. For their 121 million counterparts in the private sector, it is $49,500.[8]

Beginning in the 1970s, however, the government pivoted away from supporting itself. Even though government spending continued to increase, both in absolute terms and as a percentage of total national production, the government didn't necessarily expand its own bureaucracy by directly hiring employees.[9] Instead, massive numbers of contracts were issued to the private sector to do what the government itself had done previously. These subsidies for the corporate sector altered the economic underpinnings of this middle stratum. Out of this eventually emerged a new level of economic and political gridlock. Government spending became its own nemesis, unable to expand except at the cost of the private sector, but without which the private sector had great difficulty existing.

This further clarifies why government support for education has been whittled away, with tuition hikes and student loans used to cover what the public sector no longer can. Higher education is not quite "public" in the traditional sense of the word, but it hasn't been "privatized" either. Like the economy itself, which is part government-funded and part privately owned, higher education has become its own unique mishmash of these two realms.

Higher education cannot exist without continuing government support, a situation that is true for virtually every sector of the economy. Even *with* governmental support, stagnation seems to have overtaken the field of education, which has already privatized about as much of its operations as profitable. Enrollment and graduation rates have stalled, and the participation of some groups, whites and blacks alike, is on the decline. These may prove to be temporary setbacks, but the overall picture is similar to developments within the workworld, where stagnating wages are pervasive despite the various mechanisms deployed to spur the economy, such as infrastructure spending, new wars, tax incentives, and tax cuts.

The need to work while attending school is true for most students, even some of whom enrolled in residential colleges. At both two- and four-year institutions, 40 percent of full-time students have jobs, as do approximately 75 percent of part-time students.[10] Yet working often means attending school part-time, and both of these factors function academically as handicaps. They alter the standard time frame for degree completion, based as this is on full-time and continuous attendance.[11]

Higher education has become a type of warehousing for the underemployable, whereby the academically gifted among the potentially unemployed are transformed instead into the underemployed. Many students—for example, those already working—find themselves in this predicament even before they graduate. Another way to gauge this is to examine the life circumstances of older students, the one-third of all undergraduates who are over the age of 25. For them, dreams are measured by the distance between abilities and aspirations on the one side and actual circumstances on the other.[12] Dreams deferred motivate their college attendance and sustain them through the long years of degree attainment.

Employment alternatives

Estimates of future employment possibilities are not promising. The U.S. Bureau of Labor Statistics calculates that only three of the top ten occupations that are anticipated to produce the largest number of new jobs between 2016 and 2026 will require a bachelor's degree. Other top growth areas include personal care aides, food preparation and serving workers (including fast food), home health aides, janitors, and cleaners, all of which have median annual wages of $24,990 or less. This equals to $12 per hour for a full-time, year-round employee. The biggest growth area is personal care assistants, with 777,600 new positions anticipated.[13] Economic growth and substandard wages are synonymous. Low levels of unemployment mean only that the misery of the employed has become more widespread.

Only one out of five jobs required a four-year college degree in 2010: 15.5 percent of them a bachelor's, 1.4 percent a master's, and 3.1 percent a doctoral or professional degree. This proportion is expected to grow, but not nearly enough to absorb existing and future college graduates.[14] Viewed in still another way, the top ten technology companies who, combined, account for one-twentieth of the nation's gross domestic product employ half as few (1.5 million) as graduate each year with a bachelor's or graduate degree (2.8 million). With associate's degrees included, the total is 3.8 million graduates per year.[15] Technology is not the answer.

For the underemployed, there is simply nowhere to go. They confront a situation in which upward mobility is foreclosed. College degrees do not automatically open up career paths, despite the common belief that they do. Said one graduate, whose current position as an administrative assistant does not require a four-year degree, "I just assumed that jobs would be available with my diploma. I had done everything right academically, including a near-perfect grade point average. I was shocked by how closed the world turned out to be."

But to aim downward involves a new set of financial risks. To do anything about the future means additional resources. Almost everything except the bottom rung of jobs requires some sort of specific training and state-approved licenses. The highest rung necessitates graduate-level education, as is the case for lawyers and doctors. Active preparation for these professions begins as an undergraduate in terms of grades earned and specific prerequisite courses mastered. Baccalaureate-level licenses, like nursing or teaching, also require specific programs of study.

For licenses that require less education, their pursuit, when you already possess a bachelor's degree, constitutes a form of downward mobility. Medical assistants, among the top ten growth areas, interact with doctors and patients, use medical equipment, and conduct tests. An advanced certificate or an appropriate associate's degree is a prerequisite, even though average salaries of $32,480 are pegged at the living wage threshold. For a criminal justice major to become a paralegal, to take another example, two additional semesters of coursework may be necessary.

The skilled trades, whose members were once considered something of a "labor aristocracy" because of their decent incomes and job security, are also out of bounds for college graduates. Skilled occupations, as in precision machinery, require multi-year commitments and entail apprenticeships, classroom learning, and on-the-job experience in order to accumulate the necessary level of expertise. Becoming a licensed electrician requires an apprenticeship that lasts four to five years. After four years of college, how feasible is that?

In highly visible fields, like self-employed electricians and plumbers, small-scale contractors, firefighters, and police officers, family connections often matter because they serve as conduits to job openings.[16] One college graduate was offered a position selling specialty automotive parts because his father had gone to high school with the business owner. In many respects, this represents an updated version of the father-son and mother-daughter traditions that were once so prevalent within the factory system and in household service.

Family and friend connections are ubiquitous throughout all areas of employment, and while extremely helpful for individuals, such connections serve to reinforce the rigidities of class, race, ethnicity, and gender that typify the business arena. Prejudicial mechanisms, for instance, are ubiquitous throughout the domain of small businesses, where staff are employed solely at the discretion of the business owner. In other, larger workplaces, harassment often takes place anonymously.[17]

Only 40 percent, some 30 million out of a total of 75 million employees without a four-year degree, have what can be considered a "good job." These pay "$35,000 ($17 per hour for a full-time job) as a minimum for those under age 45 and $45,000 ($22 per hour for a full-time job) for workers age 45 and older."[18] This is the group that underemployed college graduates are encouraged to join, as witnessed in the periodic push by politicians and policy makers to increase funding for vocational training. But these areas are already overcrowded.

Employment within the "gig" economy, because it is either part-time or temporary, is itself a form of downward mobility, even when the employment requires advanced education and pays well. In the computer and high-tech industries, lucrative short-term employment leaves employees without access to employer-run continuing education. In cutting-edge fields, skills become outdated rapidly, in part because new college-educated entrants into the workforce have proficiencies that are more up to date.

A year or two represents a huge difference when technology evolves at rapid rates. As universities continue to produce an abundance of talented and eager-to-work individuals, labor shortages tend to be short-term because the collegiate system has become so adept at responding to employer needs.

For many college graduates, peripheral employment necessitates ongoing subsidies from their families. This is especially true in the creative arts. One in five underemployed college graduates finds work in food and transportation services. For customers, it can be quite pleasant to quip with your barista about philosophy, but the baristas seem to enjoy it less, the longer they are employed. The upscale restaurant business is notorious for its well-educated floor staff. Intermittent schedules work to the benefit of both employers and employees, but except for weekend evenings, wages remain low and working conditions strenuous and unpleasant. Thus, "having a college degree is only partly about obtaining access to high-paying managerial and technology jobs—it is also about beating out less educated workers for barista and clerical-type jobs."[19]

The future in education

The underemployed are trapped by the educational system, not able to advance upward because of the lack of appropriate positions, but not able to move downward either without gambling their future even further to that very same educational system. College graduates may think in terms of holding patterns, big breaks, and the near-future, but their world is dissolving, at some moments faster than at others.

Additional education entails additional debt and time spent away from the workforce. A second undergraduate degree in an area with high rates of employability and compensation is one possibility. Graduate school is another. But here too, the situation has grown murky over the past years. Some fields, like law, are on the decline due to exorbitant costs and low placement rates. One in four newly graduated lawyers are either unemployed or employed only part-time.[20]

The cannibalization of undergraduate education is already under way. This is true of graduate business education, a huge growth area. While undergraduate business management majors face underutilization rates (un- and underemployment) of 65 percent, graduate business programs have blossomed, with a proliferation of new programs and concentrations tailored to specific populations. Besides the full-time and part-time MBA programs, there are executive programs geared to working professionals that offer courses on weekends, mini-MBA programs, and focused curricula in taxation, auditing, financial computation, human resource management, hospitality services, and dozens of other specializations. There's even an online MBA in Christian Ministry.[21]

In graduate public administration, another huge growth area, undergraduates aren't jeopardized, if only because the field has few roots on that level. Public administration has grown by means of an extensive re-credentialing aimed at the already employed. Government employees and the staff at nonprofit and nongovernmental organizations are the specific focus. With stagnant growth in the public sector, however, employment for the newly credentialed opens only when incumbents leave their positions. Otherwise, they are funneled into the low-wage nonprofit and nongovernmental sectors.[22] Either way, re-credentialing produces underemployment of one sort or another.

Even when high key technology areas like mathematics, engineering, and computer science do not produce further underemployment, their existence depends on it. Each area attracts large numbers of international students, over half their graduate population in fact. Enrollment is prompted by the lack of advanced educational facilities in the countries from which the students hail, or a lack of jobs should they return.[23]

The United States has become a magnet for top students from around the globe, students with backgrounds in the upper economic strata of their own countries. Not just in the United States, but globally, to excel academically presupposes material conditions that foster excellence—outstanding schools in childhood and adolescence, highly trained and motivated teachers, tutors and other academically oriented enrichment activities, college-educated parents, and finally, family wealth sufficient to help fund these many institutions, personnel, and activities.

Reality increasingly resembles the divided society described by Marx. Social perceptions are realigning accordingly. The beliefs generated by the prosperous economy during the decades following World War II in which government spending, an expansive collegiate system, and the spawning of a self-perceived middle class have given way to a complicated and convoluted reality. How ironic that a college education, now that it has become so common and also so important to the population at large, has evolved into a defining characteristic of the educated underclass, the new working class in contemporary terms.

The mechanisms creating the new working class aren't much different from those that kept re-creating it in the past. To be born near the bottom or the top of the income and wealth spectrums increases dramatically your chances of remaining nearby throughout your life. For everyone else in the vast middle, intense pressure and frequent movement up and down the income spectrum ultimately result in very little change at all. Temporary fluctuations can be quite dramatic, but generally not long lasting enough to permanently alter your life circumstances.[24] Stagnation and near-stagnation have engulfed 80 percent of the population for three generations already.[25]

Capitalism produces more intelligence than it can use. It's what drives modern-day culture and the creative arts. How much more lively and enlivening society might be if these were the endpoints to which material resources were oriented. The promise of upward mobility is in any case mostly a mechanism to maintain social position from one generation to the next, a circumstance that pertains primarily to the one-fifth of students from comfortable backgrounds and who attend full-time residential colleges. All the rest are part of the whirlwind trying to separate false from real promises regarding the future.

The role of students in society has confounded observers ever since the expansion of the collegiate system in the post-World War II era. This coincided with the confusion regarding the place of government within an economy based on the private ownership of resources. Naming conventions are themselves scattershot endeavors. There's the educated underclass, but also the precariat and the multitude, definitions based as much on demographics and cultural attributes as on economic circumstances.[26]

Beginning in the 1960s, students have been catalysts, sometimes on their own and sometimes along with other social groups, of upheavals that have shaken the foundation of the existing order. But whereas students were once seen as separate from the working class, there's no need to continue that distinction. Appearances have changed, even though the underlying mechanisms and outcomes remain all too familiar. For college students to find the working class, they need merely to glance in a mirror.

Notes

Introduction

1. Paul Mattick, Jr., *Theory as Critique: Essays on "Capital"* (Brill, 2018), p. 196.
2. Karl Marx, *Capital, Volume 1* (Penguin, 1990 [1867]), p. 541.
3. J. H. Clapham, *The Economic Development of France and Germany, 1815–1914* (Cambridge University Press, 1968 [1936]); David Landes, *The Unbound Prometheus* (Cambridge University Press, 1969), p. 479.
4. Lawrence Mishel, Josh Bivens, Elise Gould, and Heidi Shierholz, *The State of Working America*, twelfth edition (Cornell University Press, 2012), p. 173.
5. Richard Freeman, *The Overeducated American* (Academic Press, 1976), p. 4.
6. For instance: Alec Ross, *The Industries of the Future* (Simon & Schuster, 2016).
7. An outstanding example: Ann Mullen, *Degrees of Inequality: Culture, Class, and Gender in American Higher Education* (Johns Hopkins University Press, 2010).
8. For instance: Alfred Lubrano, *Limbo: Blue-Collar Roots, White-Collar Dreams* (John Wiley and Sons, 2004).
9. Privately owned (prep) schools and institutions of higher education continued as male preserves long after the lower, elementary levels of the public education system hired women as teachers: National Center for Education Statistics (NCES), *Digest of Education Statistics: 2017*, http://nces.ed.gov, Table 318.10.
10. Michael Greenstone and Adam Looney, "Reduced Earnings for Men in America", www.brookings.edu, July 27, 2011.

11. U.S. Census Bureau, 'Married-Couple Families with Wives' Earnings Greater than Husbands' Earnings: 1981 to 2017', Table F-22, www.census.gov, August 21, 2018.

1 Higher education and class

1. National Center for Education Statistics (NCES), *Digest of Education Statistics: 2017*, http://nces.ed.gov, Table 302.60.
2. Jennifer Ma, Matea Pender, and Meredith Welch, "Education Pays 2016: The Benefits of Higher Education for Individuals and Society," http://trends.collegeboard.org, p. 14.
3. As of September 2018, 41.5 percent. Figures represent a twelve-month average: Jaison R. Abel, Richard Deitz, and Yaqin Su, "Are Recent College Graduates Finding Good Jobs?," *Current Issues in Economics and Finance*, 20:1 (2014); this data has been updated in: Federal Reserve Bank of New York, *The Labor Market for Recent College Graduates*, October 24, 2018, www.newyorkfed.org.
4. Twenty percent equals 32 million employees; see David Weil, *The Fissured Workplace* (Harvard University Press, 2014), p. 272. Also: U.S. Government Accountability Office, "Contingent Workforce: Size, Characteristics, Earnings, and Benefits," April 20, 2015 (Washington DC, 2015); U.S. Bureau of Labor Statistics, "Contingent and Alternative Employment Arrangements Summary," www.bls.gov, June 7, 2018; Marcela Escobari and Sandy Fernandez, "Measuring American Gig Workers Is Difficult, But Essential," www.brookings.edu, July 19, 2018.
5. Despite the numerous accounts of how they became wealthy, there is little information as to who they are. Thus, information on the super-rich tends to the anecdotal. See Robert Frank, *Richistan: A Journey through the American Wealth Boom and the Lives of the New Rich* (Crown Publishing Group, 2007) and the film documentaries, *Untold Wealth* (CNBC, 2008) about the newly enriched, and *Born Rich* (Shout Factory, 2003) for inherited wealth.
6. Samuel Bowles and Herbert Gintis, *Schooling in Capitalist America: Educational Reform and the Contradictions of Economic Life* (Routledge & Kegan Paul, 1976), p. 5.

7. "National data correlation between family income and educational success start in 1972": Michael Hout and Alexander Janus, "Educational Mobility in the United States Since the 1930s", in Greg J. Duncan and Richard J. Murnane, eds., *Whither Opportunity?: Rising Inequality, Schools, and Children's Life Chances* (Russell Sage Foundation, 2011), p. 167.

8. It is unclear what percent of the "high school only" subsequently earn occupational certificates, which if significant would alter our understanding of the educational pipeline: NCES, *Digest of Education Statistics: 2017*, https://nces.ed.gov, Tables 219.10, 104.10, 302.10.

9. NCES, *Digest of Education Statistics: 2017*, https://nces.ed.gov, Table 303.25.

10. Figures represent the median (midpoint) annual earnings of full-time year-round employees aged 25–34 by educational attainment in 2015. For a higher set of annual salaries, which nonetheless exhibit analogous differentials, see Ma, Pender, and Welch, "Education Pays 2016", p. 17. Neither set of data includes part-time employees and those who work less than year-round, which would alter each amount downwards significantly.

11. This survey focused on the high school class of 2004, the results of which have been used by several teams of researchers. The data was collected two years after the expected date of graduation from high school: NCES, "High School and Beyond: Overview," https://nces.ed.gov; Robert Bozick and Erich Lauff, "Education Longitudinal Study of 2002 (ELS:2002): A First Look at the Initial Postsecondary Experiences of the High School Sophomore Class of 2002," http://nces.ed.gov, October 2007, Table 3. A more recent survey of the high school class of 2013 is still in the preliminary stages and has not included information about family income; see Alexandria Walton Radford, Laura Burns Fritch, Katherine Leu, and Michael Duprey, "High School Longitudinal Study of 2009 (HSLS:09) Second Follow-Up: A First Look at Fall 2009 Ninth-Graders in 2016" (U.S. Department of Education, National Center for Education Statistics), https://nces.ed.gov, February 2018.

12. Andrew P. Kelly, "Big Payoff, Low Probability: Postsecondary Education and Upward Mobility in America," in Michael J. Petrilli. ed., *Education for Upward Mobility* (Rowman & Littlefield, 2016), p. 32.
13. This chart is based on an earlier study of high school students.
14. Claudia Goldin and Lawrence F. Katz, *The Race Between Education and Technology* (Harvard University Press, 2008), p. 260.
15. Two-thirds of the faculty at the community colleges work part-time on contracts of less than a year. At four-year institutions, however, over half the instructional staff is part-time: *The Chronicle of Higher Education: Almanac 2016–17*, August 19, 2016, pp. 13, 15.
16. Because these matters are regulated by the fifty individual states, qualifications vary considerably from place to place. This also makes it difficult to form firm assessments regarding the overall situation facing students who pursue occupational training.
17. "Certifications are issued by a non-governmental body, but licenses are awarded by a government agency and convey a legal authority to work in an occupation": U.S. Bureau of Labor Statistics, "2016 Data on Certifications and Licenses," www.bls. gov, February 9, 2018; also Tamar Jacoby, "The Certification Revolution," in *Education for Upward Mobility*, p. 55; Morris M. Kleiner, "Occupational Licensing: Protecting the Public Interest or Protectionism?," http://research.upjohn.org, 2011, p. 1.
18. NYC Healthy, "Food Protection: Online Free Training," https://www1.nyc.gov/site/doh/business/health-academy/food-protection-online-free.page; Essex County College, "Certificate of Completion in Computer-Aided Design Technology," www.essex.edu.
19. Less than one year: 44%; between one to two years: 46%: NCES, *Digest of Education Statistics: 2017*, Tables 303.25, 305.30, 318.40; Sandy Baum, Jennifer Ma, and Kathleen Payea, "Education Pays 2013: The Benefits of Higher Education for Individuals and Society," https://trends.collegeboard.org, p. 39; Arthur M. Cohen, Florence B. Brawer, and Carrie B. Kisker, *The American*

Community College, sixth edition (John Wiley & Sons, 2014), p. 314.

20. Also: Cohen, Brawer, and Kisker, *The American Community College*, p. 402.

21. From a 1930s report: "it seems probable that about 30 percent of the youth of college age among the people in the upper three deciles of economic ability go to college, less than 1 percent of those in the lowest three deciles enter college": cited in Roger L. Geiger, *The History of American Higher Education: Learning and Culture From the Founding to World War II* (Princeton University Press, 2015), p. 509. For the early 1950s, see Gabriel Kolko, *Wealth and Power in America: An Analysis of Social Class and Income Distribution* (Praeger, 1962), pp. 113–117.

22. NCES, *Digest of Education Statistics: 2017*, Table 305.30; Jennifer Ma and Sandy Baum, "Trends in Community Colleges: Enrollment, Prices, Student Debt, and Completion," http://trends.collegeboard.org, November 2015.

23. *Barron's Profiles of American Colleges: 2018*, www.barronspac.com.

24. *Barron's Profiles of American Colleges: 2018*, www.barronspac.com.

25. Derek Bok, former president of Harvard University, adds another explanation: "one practice in most selective colleges is to favor children from families wealthy enough to make a substantial donation": Derek Bok, *Higher Education in America* (Princeton University Press, 2013), p. 126; *Barron's Profiles of American Colleges: 2018*, www.barronspac.com.

26. Richard Vedder, Christopher Denhart, and Jonathan Robe, "Why Are Recent College Graduates Underemployed: University Enrollments and Labor-Market Realities," http://center forcollegeaffordability.org, January 2013, p. 27. For an analogous breakdown from 1939, see Seymour E. Harris, *The Market For College Graduates* (Harvard University Press, 1969), p. 127.

27. Figures are expressed in 2007 dollars, although they date from 1999. For more recent, but also more complicated, data, see Dirk Witteveen and Paul Attewell, "The Earnings Payoff From Attending A Selective College," *Social Science Research* 66 (2017). For an early attempt (1949) to plot education and median income

by occupational groups, see Harris, *The Market For College Graduates*, p. 39.

28. "Among 'Ivy-Plus' colleges (the eight Ivy League colleges, University of Chicago, Stanford, MIT, and Duke), more students come from families in the top 1% of the income distribution (14.5%) than the bottom half of the income distribution (13.5%)": Raj Chetty, John N. Friedman, Emmanuel Saez, Nicholas Turner, and Danny Yagan, "Mobility Report Cards: The Role of Colleges in Intergenerational Mobility," www.equality-of-opportunity.org, July 2017, Table II.

29. With slightly different data, the quote continues: "At the country's most selective schools, three percent of students come from families in the bottom economic quartile, while the top economic quartile supplies 72 percent": Tina Rosenberg, "How Colleges Can Again Be Levelers of Society," *New York Times*, May 3, 2016.

30. At public institutions, where tuition and fees are generally lower than at private colleges, the relationship between family income and elite status still holds true. Dividing attendees into quartiles yields that only 8.8 percent in the lowest-income group attend the "very selective" public institutions, whereas 19.4 percent do so from the highest-income families. At the "least selective and open admission" publics, 29.4 percent of students grew up in low-income families, but only 11.5 percent are from high-income families: Jason Delisle and Kim Dancy, "Do State Subsidies for Public Universities Favor the Affluent?," www.brookings.edu, July 28, 2016.

31. Thomas J. Espenshade and Alexandria Walton Radford, *No Longer Separate, Not Yet Equal: Race and Class in Elite College Admission and Campus Life* (Princeton University Press, 2009), p. 19.

32. See: Annette Lareau, *Unequal Childhoods: Class, Race, and Family Life* (University of California Press, 2011).

33. Greg J. Duncan and Richard J. Murnane, "Introduction: The American Dream, Then and Now," in *Whither Opportunity*, p. 11.

34. "Forty-three percent of the total endowment across all the 1,300 or so private colleges in the United States that issue bachelor's

degrees is held by just ten schools": Peter Cappelli, *Will College Pay Off?: A Guide to the Most Important Financial Decision You'll Ever Make* (Public Affairs, 2015), p. 24.

35. Carnevale and Strohl, "How Increasing College Access Is Increasing Inequality', p. 127.

36. At the lowest tier of schools, the socioeconomic differential is 18 percentage points (40 vs. 58 percent); Carnevale and Strohl, "How Increasing College Access Is Increasing Inequality," p. 150; for graduation rates by institutional selectivity, see College Board, *Trends in College Pricing: 2013*, http://trends.collegeboard.org, p. 35.

37. Isabel V. Sawhill, "Overview," in Julia B. Isaacs, Isabel V. Sawhill, and Ron Haskins, *Getting Ahead or Losing Ground: Economic Mobility in America*, www.pewtrusts.org, February 2008.

38. Espenshade and Radford, *No Longer Separate, Not Yet Equal*, p. 16.

39. For a summary of this data, see Bok, *Higher Education in America*, p. 124.

40. "The educational system legitimates economic inequality by providing an open, objective, and ostensibly meritocratic mechanism for assigning individuals to unequal economic positions": Bowles and Gintis, *Schooling in Capitalist America*, p. 103.

41. "The rhetoric of meritocracy appears to have camouflaged the extent to which success and failure often hinge decisively on events completely beyond any individual's control": Robert H. Frank, *Success and Luck: Good Fortune and the Myth of Meritocracy* (Princeton University Press, 2016), p. xii.

42. Ma, Pender, and Welch, "Education Pays 2016," p. 14, contains slightly altered figures for 1950.

43. For the entire adult population (not just 25–34 year-olds):

> 8th grade or less: 5.5%
> Some high school, no diploma: 7.3%
> High-school diploma: 27.6%
> Some college, no degree: 20.7%
> Associate degree: 8.2%
> Bachelor's degree: 19.0%

Master's degree: 8.2%
Doctoral degree: 1.4%
Professional degree: 2.0%

From "Educational Attainment of Adults (highest level)," *Chronicle of Higher Education Almanac: 2017–18*, August 18, 2017, p. 73.

2   The overproduction of intelligence

1. Jaison R. Abel, Richard Deitz, and Yaqin Su, "Are Recent College Graduates Finding Good Jobs?," *Current Issues in Economics and Finance*, 20:1 (2014), p. 1; this data has been updated in Federal Reserve Bank of New York, *The Labor Market for Recent College Graduates*, October 24, 2018, www.newyorkfed.org. Other estimates of collegiate underemployment range from 25–48 percent, with similar variations for previous decades; see the literature summary in Stephen J. Rose, "Mismatch: How Many Workers with a Bachelor's Degree Are Overqualified for Their Jobs?," www.urban.org, February 2017, pp. 29–30 and References.
2. Richard Vedder, "For Many, College Isn't Worth It," www.inside-highered.com, January 20, 2011.
3. 55.9 percent, as recorded in Janelle Jones and John Schmitt, "A College Degree is No Guarantee," http://cepr.net, May 2014, p. 5.
4. This level of scrutiny is possible because the government can now coordinate information compiled from the federal financial aid process, tax data, and other mandatory educational reports. Income data pertains to previous recipients of federal financial aid only: U.S. Department of Education, *College Scorecard*, https://collegescorecard.ed.gov/, March 29, 2018.
5. Six months post-graduation, only 34.4 percent of associate degree and 58.4 percent of bachelor's degree recipients held a full-time job of some sort, according to a survey by the National Association of Colleges and Employers, "First Destinations for the College Class of 2015," www.naceweb.org, June 2016, pp. 7, 9. Also, 15 percent of college graduates only work part-time: Abel, Deitz, and Su, "Are Recent College Graduates Finding

Good Jobs?," p. 5. Useful background is also provided in Neeta P. Fogg and Paul E. Harrington, "The Employment and Mal-Employment Situation for Recent College Graduates: An Update," www.gwcrcre.org, June 2012.

6. Federal Reserve Bank, *The Labor Market for Recent College Graduates: Underemployed Job Types.*

7. Richard Vedder, Christopher Denhart, and Jonathan Robe, "Why Are Recent College Graduates Underemployed?: University Enrollments and Labor-Market Realities," http://centerfor collegeaffordability.org, January 2013, Table 1.

8. Federal Reserve Bank, *The Labor Market for Recent College Graduates: Unemployment.*

9. Federal Reserve Bank, *The Labor Market for Recent College Graduates: Labor Market Outcomes of College Graduates by Major,* January 12, 2018.

10. This aspect of debt is missing from David Graeber, *Debt: The First 5,000 Years* (Melville House, 2011).

11. "Glossary, Repayment Period", U.S. Department of Education, Office of Federal Student Aid, www.studentloans.gov.

12. Susan Lounsbury and Lisa Cowan, "SREB Fact Book on Higher Education: U.S. Regions and 50 States in Perspective," www.sreb. org, September 2015, pp. 102, 105, 110.

13. Peter Cappelli, *Will College Pay Off?: A Guide to the Most Important Financial Decision You'll Ever Make* (Public Affairs, 2015), p. 141.

14. William Zumeta, David W. Breneman, Patrick M. Callan, and Joni E. Finney, *Financing American Higher Education in the Era of Globalization* (Harvard Education Press, 2012), p. 78.

15. Beth Akers, "How Much Is Too Much?: Evidence on Financial Well-Being and Student Loan Debt," www.aei.org, May 2014, p. 4.

16. Per debtor. In 2012, the total per debtor exceeded $26,000; per student (which includes students with no loan debt), the amount was $14,300: Tara Siegel Bernard and Ken Russell, "The New Toll of American Student Debt in 3 Charts," *New York Times,* July 11, 2018; "Average Total Debt Levels of Bachelor's-Degree Recipients at Public Four-year Colleges, 2001–2 to 2011–12,"

Chronicle of Higher Education Almanac: 2014–15, August 22, 2014, p. 37.

17. Akers, "How Much Is Too Much?," pp. 1, 8–10; Beth Akers and Matthew M. Chingos, "Is a Student Loan Crisis on the Horizon?," www.brookings.edu, June 2014; Adam Looney and Constantine Yannelis, "A Crisis in Student Loans? How Changes in the Characteristics of Borrowers and in the Institutions They Attended Contributed to Rising Loan Defaults," www.brookings.edu, Fall 2015.

18. For a brief history of mobility studies, see Michael Hout, "How Inequality May Affect Intergenerational Mobility," in Kathryn M. Neckerman, ed., *Social Inequality* (Russell Sage Foundation, 2004).

19. When wealth (real estate, stocks and bonds, automobiles, and other material goods) is used as a measure of stratification rather than income, the results are similar: Ron Haskins, "Wealth and Economic Mobility," in Julia B. Isaacs, Isabel V. Sawhill, and Ron Haskins, *Getting Ahead or Losing Ground: Economic Mobility in America*, www.pewtrusts.org, February 2008; for the update of this volume, see "Pursuing the American Dream: Economic Mobility Across Generations," www.pewtrusts.org, July 2012; also John Marsh, *Class Dismissed: Why We Cannot Teach Or Learn Our Way Out of Inequality* (Monthly Review Press, 2011), pp. 48–55.

20. Ron Haskins, "Education and Economic Mobility," in *Getting Ahead or Losing Ground*, pp. 95–96; also see "Pursuing the American Dream", p. 6.

21. Figures in parentheses inserted into quote: Isabel V. Sawhill, "Overview," in *Getting Ahead or Losing Ground*, p. 12.

22. Also, "most Americans experience absolute upward mobility but few experience relative upward mobility": "Pursuing the American Dream," p. 9.

23. For the parents, median income is averaged from 1967–71, for the children from 1995–2002. All figures were converted into 2006 dollars because of the price-level changes during the intervening years: Julia B. Isaacs, "Economic Mobility of Families Across Generations," in *Getting Ahead or Losing Ground*, p. 16.

24. Writing at the end of the last century, "Many employees are doing quite well in today's labor market, and these people, maybe 20 percent of the labor market, succeed because they have market power that derives from scarce skills": Paul Osterman, *Securing Prosperity: The American Labor Market, How It Has Changed and What To Do About It* (Princeton University Press, 2001), p. 116.

25. For an example, Frank Parkin, "Marxism and Class Theory: A Bourgeois Critique," in Rhonda F. Levine, ed., *Social Class and Stratification: Classical Statements and Theoretical Debates*, second edition (Rowman & Littlefield, 2006); also Pierre Bourdieu, "What Makes a Social Class? On the Theoretical and Practical Existence of Groups," *Berkeley Journal of Sociology*, 32 (1987): 1–17.

26. For this discussion, I rely on Paul Mattick, Jr., *Theory as Critique: Essays on "Capital"*, Chapter 9: "Class and Capital" (Brill, 2018). Marx acknowledges that "this class articulation does not emerge in pure form" and that "middle and transitional levels always conceal the boundaries" within which there is an "infinite fragmentation of interests and positions": Karl Marx, *Capital: Volume 3* (Vintage, 1981), pp. 1025–1026.

27. For a useful overview of the many definitions of class used in the social sciences, see Richard V. Reeves, Katherine Guyot, and Eleanor Krause, "Defining The Middle Class: Cash, Credentials, or Culture?," www.brookings.edu, May 7, 2018.

28. For a depiction of social class in the form of graduated steps, see the three-dimensional diagram: "How Class Works: Income by Education", www.nytimes.com, 2005; also see the twelve definitions of middle class provided graphically in Richard V. Reeves, Katherine Guyot, and Eleanor Krause, "A Dozen Ways To Be Middle Class," www.brookings.edu, May 8, 2018.

29. Similarly, nearly 20 percent of men aged 25–34 with a bachelor's degree earned less than the average high school graduate. Among women, the figure was 14 percent: John Schmitt and Heather Boushey, "The College Conundrum: Why the Benefits of a College Education May Not Be So Clear, Especially to Men," www.americanprogress.org, December 2010, pp. 2–3.

30. Anthony P. Carnevale and Jeff Strohl, "How Increasing College Access Is Increasing Inequality, and What to Do about It," in Richard D. Kahlenberg, ed., *Rewarding Strivers: Helping Low-Income Students Succeed in College* (Century Foundation Press, 2010), p. 71.
31. Andrew J. Cherlin, *Labor's Love Lost: The Rise and Fall of the Working-Class Family in America* (Russell Sage Foundation, 2014), p. 127.
32. Tamara Draut, *Sleeping Giant: How the New Working Class Will Transform America* (Anchor Books, 2016), p. 6.
33. Draut, *Sleeping Giant*, p. 5.
34. Kevin T. Leicht and Scott T. Fitzgerald, *Middle Class Meltdown in America: Causes, Consequences, and Remedies* (Routledge, 2014), pp. 15–16.
35. Earl Wysong, Robert Perrucci, and David Wright, *The New Class Society: Goodbye American Dream?*, fourth edition (Rowman & Littlefield, 2014), pp. 23, 31, 33. A British research team identified seven social classes: Mike Savage, *Social Class in the 21st Century* (Penguin, 2015), p. 174. For a comparison of three different typologies, see Wikipedia, "Social Class in the United States: Academic Models," https://en.wikipedia.org.

3 Class in transition: historical background

1. Paul Mattick, *Marx and Keynes: The Limits of the Mixed Economy* (Porter Sargent, 1969), p. 150.
2. "In 1862, Congress passed the Morrill Act encouraging the establishment of public land-grant universities" and "required the institutions to focus on teaching agriculture and the mechanical arts, but it did not preclude the teaching of classics as well":. Steven J. Diner, *Universities and their Cities: Urban Higher Education in America* (Johns Hopkins University Press, 2017), p. 9.
3. National Center for Education Statistics (NCES), *Digest of Education Statistics: 2017*, Table 303.10.
4. NCES, *Digest of Education Statistics: 2017*, Tables 214.30, 305.30; Michael Paris, "Boards of Education," in Stephen L. Schechter (ed.), *American Governance* (Macmillan, 2016).

5. Alia Wong, "The Downfall of For-Profit Colleges," www.the atlantic.com, February 23, 2015; Gregory D. Kutz, "For-Profit Colleges: Undercover Testing Finds Colleges Encouraged Fraud and Engaged in Deceptive and Questionable Marketing Practices," www.gao.gov. For a breakdown of revenue at public institutions: Susan Lounsbury and Lisa Cowan, "SREB Fact Book on Higher Education: U.S. Regions and 50 States in Perspective," www.sreb.org, September 2015, pp. 168–169; William Zumeta, David W. Breneman, Patrick M. Callan, and Joni E. Finney, *Financing American Higher Education in the Era of Globalization* (Harvard Education Press, 2012), pp. 17, 20.

6. "ITT Educational Services Files for Bankruptcy After Aid Crackdown," *New York Times*, September 17, 2016; Charles Huckabee, "Corinthian Colleges Inc. to Close Its Remaining Campuses," *Chronicle of Higher Education*, April 27, 2015.

7. NCES, *Digest of Education Statistics: 2017*, Table 317.50.

8. Per student funding has declined, not necessarily the total appropriation: Phil Oliff, Vincent Palacios, Ingrid Johnson, and Michael Leachman, "Recent Deep State Higher Education Cuts May Harm Students and the Economy for Years to Come," www. cbpp.org, March 19, 2013, pp. 1–2, 21.

9. Less than 5 percent of adults had a four-year degree, although a slightly larger group had attended but without graduating: Seymour E. Harris, *A Statistical Portrait of Higher Education* (McGraw-Hill, 1972), pp. 412–413, 418; Ivar Berg, *Education and Jobs: The Great Training Robbery* (Percheron Press, 1972), p. 64; Roger L. Geiger, *The History of American Higher Education: Learning and Culture From the Founding to World War II* (Princeton University Press, 2015), p. 515.

10. Robert J. Gordon, *The Rise and Fall of American Growth: The U.S. Standard of Living Since the Civil War* (Princeton University Press, 2016), p. 53.

11. Steve Fraser, *The Age of Acquiescence: The Life and Death of American Resistance to Organized Wealth and Power* (Little, Brown, 2015), p. 327; also Richard A. Walker, *Pictures of a Gone City: Tech and the Dark Side of Prosperity in the San Francisco Bay Area* (PM Press, 2018), pp. 132–134.

12. Claudia Goldin and Lawrence F. Katz, *The Race Between Education and Technology* (Harvard University Press, 2008), pp. 102, 105 (quote), 106, 113.
13. George Soule, *Prosperity Decade: From War to Depression, 1917–1929* (Holt, Rinehart and Winston, 1964), Chapter XIII.
14. Keith W. Olson, *The G.I. Bill, the Veterans, and the Colleges* (University Press of Kentucky, 1974), pp. 23–24, 59, 72, 76; John R. Thelin, *A History of American Higher Education*, second edition (Johns Hopkins University Press, 2011), pp. 262–263; Kathleen J. Frydl, *The GI Bill* (Cambridge University Press, 2009), p. 308.
15. Olson, *The G.I. Bill*, pp. 47–48; Seymour E. Harris, *The Market for College Graduates* (Harvard University Press, 1969), p. 175.
16. Frydl, *The GI Bill*, p. 307.
17. Mattick, *Marx & Keynes*, Chapters 9, 11–14.
18. Public institutions of higher education added 1,744 buildings between the four years spanning 1951 to 1955. A third of current campus space was built during the 1960s and '70s: Frydl, *The GI Bill*, p. 318; Harris, *A Statistical Portrait of Higher Education*, pp. 718–721; "State of Facilities in Higher Education: 2016 Benchmarks, Best Practices, and Trends,", www.sightlines.com, p. 7. NCES, *Digest of Education Statistics: 2017*, Table 301.20.
19. Richard B. Freeman, *The Overeducated American* (Academic Press, 1976), pp. 1–2.
20. Freeman, *The Overeducated American*, p. 20.
21. *Historical Statistics of the United States*, D: 139–41.
22. Measured in 1982 dollars, GNP increased from $1203.7 billion to $2416.6 billion between 1950 and 1970. Spending for higher education increased from 1.0 percent of GNP to 2.7 percent; for education in general from 3.4 to 7.5 percent, before declining slightly and then leveling off for the next two decades: Charles J. Andersen, Deborah J. Carter, Andrew G. Malizio, and Bolichi San, *1989–90 Fact Book on Higher Education* (American Council on Education, 1989), pp. 48–49; Arthur M. Cohen, Florence B. Brawer, and Carrie B. Kisker, *The American Community College*, sixth edition (John Wiley & Sons, 2014), p. 153.
23. Michael French, *US Economic History Since 1945* (Manchester University Press, 1997), p. 84.

24. Goldin and Katz, *The Race Between Education and Technology*, p. 168.
25. Richard Vedder, "For Many, College Isn't Worth It," www.insidehighered.com, January 20, 2011.
26. Gordon, *The Rise and Fall of American Growth*, pp. 5, 357, 382, 416.
27. Andrew J. Cherlin, *Labor's Love Lost: The Rise and Fall of the Working-Class Family in America* (Russell Sage Foundation, 2014), pp. 1, 26.
28. For a seminal piece, see Kathy Stone, "The Origin of Job Structures in the Steel Industry," in *Root & Branch: The Rise of the Workers Movements* (Fawcett Crest, 1975), pp. 123–158.
29. Randall Collins, *The Credential Society: An Historical Sociology of Education and Stratification* (Academic Press, 1979), p. 3.
30. Richard Sennett and Jonathan Cobb, *The Hidden Injuries of Class* (W.W. Norton, 1993 [1972]), p. 74.
31. Daniel Bell, *The End of Ideology* (Harvard University Press, 1988 [1960]); André Gorz, *Farewell to the Working Class* (Pluto Press, 1999 [1980]).
32. For a discussion of these issues from the perspective of academic sociology, see Michael Hout, "How Class Works: Objective and Subjective Aspects of Class Since the 1970s," in Annette Lareau and Dalton Conley (eds.), *Social Class: How Does It Work?* (Russell Sage Foundation, 2008); also Mike Savage, *Social Class in the 21ˢᵗ Century* (Penguin, 2015), pp. 25–26.
33. Ira Katznelson, *When Affirmative Action Was White: An Untold History of Racial Inequality in Twentieth-Century America* (W.W. Norton, 2005), especially Chapter 5.
34. Including families in which either only one or both parents had "some college" but had not graduated, accounted for over two-thirds (71 percent) of the student body: Bureau of Social Science Research, *Two Years After the College Degree* (U.S. Government Printing Office, 1963), p. 18.
35. Gorz, *Farewell to the Working Class*, p.75.
36. Studs Terkel, *Working: People Talk About What They Do All Day and How They Feel About What They Do* (New Press, 2004); Reeve

Vanneman and Lynn Weber Cannon, *The American Perception of Class* (Temple University Press, 1987), p. 1.

37. *All in the Family*, *The Jeffersons*, *Law and Order*, https://en.wikipedia.org.

38. Sandy Baum, Charles Kurose, and Jennifer Ma, "How College Shapes Lives: Understanding the Issues,", http://trends.college board.org, October 2013, p. 36; also Stephen J. Rose, "Mismatch: How Many Workers with a Bachelor's Degree Are Overqualified for Their Jobs?" www.urban.org, February 2017, pp. 8–9, 25 for higher estimates.

39. Hout, "How Class Works', pp. 6–7, 9–10, 30 (quote), 33–34.

40. Hout, "How Class Works', pp. 33–35.

4   Underemployment through the decades

1. Bureau of Social Science Research, *Two Years After the College Degree* (U.S. Government Printing Office, 1963), pp. 57, 61, 234–236.

2. "In 1952, 18.4% of American workers were professionals or managers, while only 7.9% had a college degree—which implies that there were 2.33 college-level jobs available per graduate workers": Richard B. Freeman, *The Overeducated American* (Academic Press, 1976), pp. 16–19. See also Carl L. Bankston III, "The Mass Production of Credentials: Subsidies and the Rise of the Higher Education Industry," *The Independent Review*, 15.3 (Winter 2011): 328–330.

3. Ever since the late 1950s, part-time students have constituted anywhere from one-third to two-fifths of all college students: National Center for Education Statistics, *Digest of Education Statistics: 2017*, http://nces.ed.gov, Table 303.10.

4. Jeffrey J. Selingo, *There Is Life After College: What Parents and Students Should Know About Navigating School to Prepare for the Jobs of Tomorrow* (HarperCollins, 2016), p. 5.

5. "Total unemployed, plus discouraged workers, plus all marginally attached workers, plus total employed part time for economic reasons, as a percent of the civilian labor force plus all marginally attached workers": Steven E. Haugen, "Measures of Labor

Underutilization from the Current Population Survey", www.
bls.gov, March 2009, p. 9. See also Julius Shiskin, "Employment
and Unemployment: The Doughnut or the Hole?", www.bls.
gov, February 1976. On data collection: Scott Keeter, "How
We Know What We Know", in Paul Taylor, *The Next America:
Boomers, Millennials, and the Looming Generational Showdown*
(Public Affairs, 2015), pp. 241–274.

6. Lawrence Mishel, Josh Bivens, Elise Gould, and Heidi Shierholz,
The State of Working America, twelfth edition (Cornell University
Press, 2012), p. 350; U.S. Bureau of Labor Statistics, "Table A-15
Alternative Measures of Labor Underutilization," www.bls.gov,
November 2, 2018.

7. "The labor force as a percent of the civilian noninstitutional
population," that is, neither incarcerated, held in a mental facility,
confined to a home for the aged, or an active member of the
armed forces: U.S. Bureau of Labor Statistics, "Glossary," www.
bls.gov, June 7, 2016; U.S. Bureau of Labor Statistics, "Labor
Force Statistics from the Current Population Survey," http://
data.bls.gov, November 2, 2018.

8. Benjamin J. Keys and Sheldon Danziger, "Hurt the Worst: The
Risk of Unemployment among Disadvantaged and Advantaged
Male Workers, 1968–2003," in Katherine S. Newman (ed.), *Laid
Off, Laid Low: Political and Economic Consequences of Employment
Insecurity* (Columbia University Press, 2008), pp. 59–61.

9. One study found that in the U.S., where "the fraction of the
population age 65 or older will rise from around 20 percent of
the working age population in 2007 to 40 percent by 2050," 40
percent of retirees, "mostly in their late 60s or 70s, are willing to
work again at the time of the survey if all the conditions are the
same as their last job, including hourly wage, total number of
hours, and type of job." With flexible schedules, this rises to 60
percent of retired responders: John Ameriks, Joseph S. Briggs,
Andrew Caplin, Minjoon Lee, Matthew D. Shapiro, and Christopher Tonetti, "Older Americans Would Work Longer If Jobs
Were Flexible," NBER Working Paper No. 24008, www.nber.
org, November 2017.

10. Wide variations existed for women and men. No more than 40 percent of women were employed full-time, year-round between 1950 and 1965, whereas for men, the average approached the 70 percent level: Dean Morse, *The Peripheral Worker* (Columbia University Press, 1969), pp. 5, 46–54, 129–132.

11. D. W. Livingstone, *The Education-Jobs Gap: Underemployment or Economic Democracy* (Westview Press, 1998), pp. xii, 84.

12. Mishel, Bivens, Gould, and Shierholz, *The State of Working America*, p. 422.

13. Barry Bluestone and Bennett Harrison, *The Deindustrialization of America: Plant Closings, Community Abandonment, and the Dismantling of Basic Industry* (Basic Books, 1982), pp. 9, 30.

14. Louis Uchitelle, *The Disposable American: Layoffs and Their Consequences* (Vintage, 2007), pp. ix, 5, 208, 212.

15. Council of Economic Advisors, "Economic Report of the President 1981," www.presidency.ucsb.edu, p. 71.

16. Census reports that include white-collar manufacturing employees add some 3–4 million to these totals. In either method of counting, the trends are the same: U.S. Census Bureau, *Statistical Abstract of the United States*, 1980.679 (Part 5, p. 406), July 23, 2015; 1990.650 (Part 4, p. 394), September 26, 2015; 2000.672 (Section 13, p. 420), October 8, 2015), www.census.gov; U.S. Bureau of Labor Statistics, "Manufacturing," http://data.bls.gov, June 30, 2018 (July dates). For a brief overview of global conditions, see Michael Roberts, "Deindustrialisation and Socialism," https://thenextrecession.wordpress.com, October 21, 2014.

17. In agriculture, crop yields between 1945 and 1989 had increased in wheat from 16.9 to 35.3 bushels per acre, in corn from 36.1 to 111.5 bushels, and in cotton from 273 to 624 lbs., while the family farm disappeared and a combination of farm machines, chemicals, and migrant labor took their place: Michael French, *US Economic History Since 1945* (Manchester University Press, 1997), p. 115.

18. As measured in 2005 dollars: Veronique de Rugy, "U.S. Manufacturing: Output vs. Jobs Since 1975," www.mercatus.org, January 24, 2011; U.S. Bureau of Labor Statistics, "Manufacturing."

19. Between 1947 and 2013, overall output in the United States increased nine-fold, even though working hours did not quite double. Between 1998 and 2013, employees worked the same number of total hours (194 billion), yet production had increased 42 percent: Shawn Sprague, "What Can Labor Productivity Tell Us About the U.S. Economy," www.bls.gov, May 2014.

20. For the transformation of the economy in the late twentieth century, see the two books by Joyce Kolko: *America and the Crisis of World Capitalism* (Beacon Press, 1974) and *Restructuring the World Economy* (Pantheon, 1988).

21. During the late 1990s, over 40 percent of union members had attended college: Gerald Mayer, "Union Membership Trends in the United States," Tables A1, A6, http://digitalcommons.ilr. cornell.edu, August 31, 2004; U.S. Bureau of Labor Statistics, "Members of Unions," https://data.bls.gov, March 26, 2017; U.S. Bureau of Labor Statistics, "Labor Force Statistics from the Current Population Survey," http://data.bls.gov, January 19, 2018.

22. Daniel E. Hecker, "Reconciling Conflicting Data on Jobs for College Graduates," *Monthly Labor Review*, July 1992, p. 10.

23. Perhaps not coincidentally, high school graduation rates rose only minimally from the early 1970s until after the turn of the new century: NCES, *Digest of Education Statistics: 2017*, http://nces. ed.gov, Table 219.65.

24. All figures converted to 2011 dollars; Mishel, Bivens, Gould, and Shierholz, *The State of Working America*, p. 215.

25. Arne L. Kalleberg, *Good Jobs, Bad Jobs: The Rise of Polarized and Precarious Employment Systems in the United States, 1970s to 2000s* (Russell Sage Foundation, 2011), pp. 29, 221 n.32.

26. For a comprehensive and personalized account, see Steven Greenhouse, *The Big Squeeze: Tough Times for the American Worker* (Knopf, 2008).

27. David Autor, "The Polarization of Job Opportunities in the U.S. Labor Market: Implications for Employment and Earnings," http://economics.mit.edu, April 2010, p. 1.

28. David Weil, *The Fissured Workplace: Why Work Became So Bad For So Many People and What Can Be Done To Improve It* (Harvard University Press, 2014), p. 49.

29. Paul Osterman, *Securing Prosperity: The American Labor Market, How It Has Changed and What To Do About It* (Princeton University Press, 2001), p. 91.

30. "The retail trade and service sectors accounted for over three-fourths of all low earners," that is, businesses that sell directly to the public and food-related establishments: Fredrik Andersson, Harry J. Holzer, and Julia I. Lane, *Moving Up or Moving On: Who Advances in the Low-Wage Labor Market?* (Russell Sage Foundation, 2005), pp. 25–26, 35–36.

31. W. Norton Grubb and Marvin Lazerson, *The Education Gospel: The Economic Power of Schooling* (Harvard University Press, 2004), p. 166.

32. Weil, *The Fissured Workplace*, pp. 7, 210.

33. "Lower-educated, younger, black, and male workers have tended to have higher job turnover over time": Neil Fligstein and Taek-Jin Shin, "The Shareholder Value Society: A Review of the Changes in Working Conditions and Inequality in the United States, 1976-2000," in Kathryn M. Neckerman (ed.), *Social Inequality* (Russell Sage Foundation, 2004), p. 406; Kalleberg, *Good Jobs, Bad Jobs*, p. 93.

34. Kalleberg, *Good Jobs, Bad Jobs*, pp. 150–151, 153; Claude S. Fischer and Michael Hout, *Century of Difference: How America Changed in the Last One Hundred Years* (Russell Sage Foundation, 2006), p. 125.

35. Also, "there has been an increase in job durations and the incidence of long-term employment relationships in the public sector, with the increase more pronounced for women": Henry S. Farber, "Short(er) Shrift: The Decline in Worker-Firm Attachment in the United States," in Newman, *Laid Off, Laid Low*, p. 11.

36. Kalleberg, *Good Jobs, Bad Jobs*, p. 48.

37. U.S. Bureau of Labor Statistics, "Table 23: Married-Couple Families by Number and Relationship of Earners, 1967–2008," www.bls.gov.

38. U.S. Bureau of Labor Statistics, "Manufacturing."

39. A peculiarity of deindustrialization literature was the discovery of economic traits, like the "mass worker," by portions of the left precisely when these phenomena were starting to pass out of existence. Other odd discoveries included "monopoly capitalism" just as the combination of new technologies and globalization was about to undermine the preexisting oligopolistic structure of industry, and "wages for housework," coincident with an era in which women were incorporated into paid work to an unprecedented degree, divorce rates soared, and single-parent households became a new norm.

40. Federal Reserve Bank of St. Louis, "Federal Debt: Total Public Debt as Percent of Gross Domestic Product," https://fred. stlouisfed.org, September 27, 2018.

41. Paul Mattick, Jr., *Business As Usual: The Economic Crisis and the Failure of Capitalism* (Reaktion Books, 2011), p. 56.

42. "History of the United States Public Debt," https://en.wikipedia. org.

43. Richard Vedder, Christopher Denhart, Matthew Denhart, Christopher Matgouranis and Jonathan Robe, "From Wall Street to Wal-Mart: Why College Graduates Are Not Getting Good Jobs," http://centerforcollegeaffordability.org, December 2010, p. 5.

44. Ron Haskins, "Education and the 'Success Sequence'," in Michael J. Petrilli (ed.), *Education for Upward Mobility* (Rowman & Littlefield, 2016), p. 13.

45. Hecker, "Reconciling Conflicting Data on Jobs for College Graduates," p. 4; Jaison R. Abel, Richard Deitz, and Yaqin Su, "Are Recent College Graduates Finding Good Jobs?," *Current Issues in Economics and Finance*, 20.1 (2014): 3.

46. Richard Freeman attempted to calculate the circumstances under which the college premium would rise or fall: "when [college] graduates were hard to obtain and cost 40% more than high school workers, enterprises preferred the latter," but when college graduates cost "just 25% more than their high school competitors, it became profitable to substitute the former": Freeman, *The Overeducated American*, p. 48.

47. John Marsh, *Class Dismissed: Why We Cannot Teach Or Learn Our Way Out of Inequality* (Monthly Review Press, 2011), p. 76.
48. Vedder, Denhart, Denhart, Matgouranis, and Robe, "From Wall Street to Wal-Mart."
49. For debates regarding the existence of college-educated under-employment, see Anthony P. Carnevale, "College is Still Worth It," www.insidehighered.com, January 14, 2011, and Richard Vedder, "For Many, College Isn't Worth It," www.insidehighered.com, January 20, 2011. For the general issue, see Peter Cappelli, "Skill Gaps, Skill Shortages, and Skill Mismatches: Evidence for the US," www.nber.org, August 2014.
50. Sandy Baum, Charles Kurose, and Jennifer Ma, "How College Shapes Lives: Understanding the Issues," http://trends.collegeboard.org, October 2013, p. 36.
51. Stephen J. Rose, "Mismatch: How Many Workers with a Bachelor's Degree Are Overqualified for Their Jobs?," www.urban.org, February 2017, p. 25.
52. "Managers were a more likely target during the 1991 to 1993 recession. Professional, technical, and sales workers also appeared to have higher rates of job loss during the 1991 to 1993 recession": Fligstein and Shin, "The Shareholder Value Society', p. 407.

5   Class status and economic instability

1. Lawrence Mishel, Josh Bivens, Elise Gould, and Heidi Shierholz, *The State of Working America*, twelfth edition (Cornell University Press, 2012), p. 427; for a summary of the literature, see John Iceland, *Poverty in America: A Handbook*, third edition (University of California Press, 2013), p. 48; also Ashley N Edwards, "Dynamics of Economic Well-Being: Poverty, 2009–2011," www.census.gov, January 2014.
2. For instance, "employers of low-wage workers protested" the Humphrey-Hawkins Full Employment Act in the late 1970s: Louis Uchitelle, *The Disposable American: Layoffs and their Consequences* (Vintage: 2007), p. 127; for the working poor, see Sarah Halpern-Meekin, Kathryn Edin, Laura Tach, and Jennifer Sykes,

It's Not Like I'm Poor: How Working Families Make Ends Meet in a Post-Welfare World (University of California Press, 2015).

3. Mishel, Bivens, Gould, and Shierholz, *The State of Working America*, p. 422; "Personal Responsibility and Work Opportunity Act," https://en.wikipedia.org; *Federal Register*, 81.15 (January 25, 2016): 4036.

4. U.S. Census Bureau, "Income and Poverty in the United States: 2017: Poverty Thresholds," www.census.gov, September 12, 2018.

5. Household variation, in contrast, is less volatile than for individuals: Congressional Budget Office, "Recent Trends in the Variability of Individual Earnings and Household Income," www.cbo.gov, June 2008, p. 7.

6. U.S. Census Bureau, "Income and Poverty in the United States: 2017," "Table A-2, Mean Household Income of Quintiles."

7. Lawrence Summers, "It Can Be Morning Again for the World's Middle Class," *Financial Times*, January 18, 2015.

8. William G. Gale, "Distribution of Federal Taxes and Income, 1979–2000," http://webarchive.urban.org, September 29, 2003.

9. Iceland, *Poverty in American*, p. 46.

10. Programs include Medicaid, Children's Health Insurance Program (CHIP), Supplemental Nutrition Assistance Program (SNAP) (food stamps), Earned Income Tax Credit (EITC), and Temporary Assistance for Needy Families (TANF). This study pre-dates the Affordable Care Act (ACA, or Obamacare): Sylvia A. Allegretto, Marc Doussard, Dave Graham-Squire, Ken Jacobs, Dan Thompson, and Jeremy Thompson, "Fast Food, Poverty Wages: The Public Cost of Low-Wage Jobs in the Fast-Food Industry," Center for Labor Research and Education brief, University of California, Berkeley, http://laborcenter.berkeley.edu, October 15, 2013, p. 1; U.S. Department of Agriculture: Food and Nutrition Service, "Supplemental Nutrition Assistance Program: Number of Persons Participating," www.fns.usda.gov, October 11, 2016.

11. Fredrik Andersson, Harry J. Holzer, and Julia I. Lane, *Moving Up or Moving On: Who Advances in the Low-Wage Labor Market?* (Russell Sage Foundation, 2005), p. 45; also Jacob S. Hacker, *The*

Great Risk Shift: The New Economic Insecurity and the Decline of the American Dream (Oxford University Press, 2008), p. 31.

12. Mishel, Bivens, Gould, and Shierholz, *The State of Working America*, p. 330; W. Norton Grubb, *Working in the Middle: Strengthening Education and Training for the Mid-Skilled Labor Force* (Jossey-Bass, 1996), p. 15.

13. Irene Tung, Yannet Lathrop, and Paul Sonn, "The Growing Movement for $15," http://nelp.org, November 2015, pp. 1–2, 6.

14. Richard Seltzer and Holona LeAnne Ochs, *Gratuity: A Contextual Understanding of Tipping Norms from the Perspective of Tipped Employees* (Rowman & Littlefield, 2010), pp. 1–2.

15. Ken Jacobs, "Americans are Spending $153 Billion."

16. Allegretto, Doussard, Graham-Squire, Jacobs, Thompson, and Thompson, "Fast Food, Poverty Wages, p. 1; Ken Jacobs, Zohar Perla, Ian Perry, and Dave Graham-Squire, "Producing Poverty: The Public Cost of Low-Wage Production Jobs in Manufacturing," http://laborcenter.berkeley.edu, pp. 3, 6, May 10, 2016.

17. Sylvia A. Allegretto, Ken Jacobs, Dave Graham-Squire, and Megan Emiko Scott, "The Public Cost of Low-Wage Jobs in the Banking Industry," http://laborcenter.berkeley.edu, October 27, 2014; U.S. Department of Labor, *Occupational Outlook Handbook, 2016–17,* "Tellers," www.bls.gov, December 17, 2017.

18. Ken Jacobs, "Americans are Spending $153 Billion a Year to Subsidize McDonald's and Wal-Mart's Low Wage Workers," http://laborcenter.berkeley.edu, April 15, 2015.

19. Also: David Weil, *The Fissured Workplace: Why Work Became So Bad For So Many and What Can Be Done To Improve It* (Harvard University Press, 2014), p. 129; U.S. Bureau of Labor Statistics, "Occupational Employment Statistics," www.bls.gov, May 2015; Steve Fraser, *The Age of Acquiescence: The Life and Death of American Resistance to Organized Wealth and Power* (Little, Brown, 2015), pp. 248–256.

20. Noam Scheiber, "Growth in the 'Gig Economy' Fuels Work Force Anxieties," *New York Times,* July 12, 2015; Fredrick Kunkle, "Uber Drivers Earn About $15.68 an Hour but Disparities are Significant, Survey Finds," *Washington Post*, January 26, 2017, www.washingtonpost.com.

21. Fed Ex, "Owner Operators: Overview/Advantages," http://customcritical.fedex.com, 2017; Weil, *The Fissured Workplace*, pp. 161–162.

22. As of December 31, 2016; Apple, "Two Million U.S. Jobs. And Counting," www.apple.com, May 2017.

23. "Apple," www.glassdoor.com.

24. "Creating Jobs Through Innovation," www.apple.com; Associated Press, "Twitter Cuts Staff, Kills Off Vine App Amid Pressure to Grow," www.cnsnews.com, October 27, 2016.

25. Ian Hathaway and Mark Muro, "Tracking the Gig Economy: New Numbers," www.brookings.edu, October 13, 2016; U.S. Census Bureau, "2016 Nonemployer Statistics," http://censtats.census.gov, June 21, 2018.

26. Federal Reserve Banks, "2015 Small Business Credit Survey: Report on Nonemployer Firms," December 2016, p. iii.

27. For the 14.6 million self-employed and their 29.4 employees: Rakesh Kochhar, "Three-in-Ten U.S. Jobs are Held by the Self-Employed and the Workers They Hire: Hiring More Prevalent Among Self-Employed Asians, Whites and Men," www.pewsocialtrends.org, October 22, 2015.

28. 2012 data. U.S. Census Bureau, "Nearly 1 in 10 Businesses With Employees Are New, According to Inaugural Annual Survey of Entrepreneurs," www.census.gov, September 1, 2016.

29. Michael Mandel, "An Analysis of Job and Wage Growth in the Tech/Telecom Sector," www.progressivepolicy.org, September 2017, p. 5.

30. Between 1970 and 2010, population increased from 203.2 to 308.7 million; the civilian labor force from 82.8 to 153.9 million; collegiate enrollments from 8.6 to 21 million. Between 2000 and 2010, population grew by 10 percent, the civilian labor force by 8 percent, and collegiate enrollments by 37 percent: U.S. Census Bureau, "Resident Population Data: Population Change, 2010 Census," www.census.gov, April 30, 2018; U.S. Bureau of Labor Statistics, "Labor Force Statistics from the Current Population Survey," http://data.bls.gov.

31. National Center for Education Statistics, *Digest of Education Statistics: 2017*, http://nces.ed.gov, Table 306.10.

32. For a quick summary, National Conference of State Legislatures, "Affirmative Action: Court Decisions," www.ncsl.org, June 2016.
33. NCES, *Digest of Education Statistics: 2017*, Tables 323.10, 324.40.
34. Association of American Medical Colleges, "Table B-5: Total Enrollment by U.S. Medical School and Race/Ethnicity, 2015–2016," www.aamc.org; NCES, *Digest of Education Statistics: 2017*, Table 324.55.
35. NCES, *Digest of Education Statistics: 2017*, Tables 315.20, 306.10.
36. Viewed in terms of tenure (that is, lifetime appointments), the same decline is evident—over 50 percent of the faculty were tenured or tenure-track in 1975, but less than a third were so designated as of 2005: NCES, *Digest of Education Statistics: 2017*, Table 315.10; Arne L. Kalleberg, "Precarious Work, Insecure Workers: Employment Relations in Transition," *American Sociological Review* 74 (February 2009): 9.
37. Goldie Blumenstyk, *American Higher Education in Crisis?: What Everyone Needs to Know* (Oxford University Press, 2015), pp. 21–22.
38. Isabel V. Sawhill, "Overview," in Julia B. Isaacs, Isabel V. Sawhill, and Ron Haskins, *Getting Ahead or Losing Ground: Economic Mobility in America*, www.pewtrusts.org, February 2008, p. 8.
39. Richard V. Reeves, *Dream Hoarders: How the American Upper Middle Class Is Leaving Everyone Else in the Dust, Why That Is a Problem, and What to Do About It* (Brookings Institution, 2017).
40. Households and families are referred to as interchangeable in Emmanuel Saez and Gabriel Zucman, "Wealth Inequality in the United States since 1913: Evidence from Capitalized Income Tax Data," p. 12, Table 1, October 2014, http://eml.berkeley.edu.
41. U.S. Census Bureau, "Quarterly Residential Vacancies and Homeownership, First Quarter 2018," www.census.gov, April 26, 2018.
42. See also Citigroup, "Time to Re-Commit to Plutonomy Stocks—Binge on Bling," *The Global Investigator*, September 29, 2006, p. 11.
43. In 2014 dollars: Pew Research Center, "The American Middle Class is Losing Ground," p. 9.

44. The top 20 percent of families account for 84 percent of these wealth transfers: Edward N. Wolff, *Inheriting Wealth in America: Future Boom or Bust?* (Oxford University Press, 2015), pp. 3–5, 81.

45. For the period 2005–09: Patrick Wightman, Megan Patrick, Robert Schoeni, and John Schulenberg, "Historical Trends in Parental Financial Support of Young Adults," www.psc.isr, September 2013, pp. 5, 23, 33.

46. Robert Frank, "More Millionaires Than Ever Are Living in the US," www.cnbc.com, March 10, 2015.

47. *Forbes*, "Two Decades of CEO Pay," www.forbes.com, December 2012; "100 Highest Paid CEOs', www.aflcio.org.

48. The median household wealth for whites is $141,900, for blacks $11,000, for latinx $13,700: Chuck Collins and Josh Hoxie, "Billionaire Bonanza Report: The Forbes 400 ... and the Rest of Us," www.ips-dc.org, December 2015, pp. 1, 5, 6.

49. They also charted households by the number of members. Thus, a two-person middle-income household ranged from $34,186 to $102,560, whereas a four-person middle-income household included those between $48,347 and $145,041: Pew Research Center, "The American Middle Class is Losing Ground: No Longer the Majority and Falling Behind Financially," www.pewsocialtrends.org, December 9, 2015, pp. 6–7, 16–17; for similar studies, see Alicia Parlapiano, Robert Gebeloff, and Shan Carter, "The Shrinking Middle Class," www.nytimes.com, January 26, 2015; Richard V. Reeves and Edward Rodrigue, "The American Middle-Class is Still Thriving in Utah," www.brookings.edu, March 10, 2016.

50. Thomas A. Hirschl and Mark R. Rank, "The Life Course Dynamics of Affluence," *PLoS ONE* 10.1 (January 2015): 5–6, journals.plos.org.

6 Into the future

1. Nearly 40 percent of 22–24 year-olds now live at home: Richard Arum and Josipa Roksa, *Aspiring Adults Drift: Tentative Transitions of College Graduates* (University of Chicago Press, 2014),

pp. 85–87; Richard Fry, "More Millennials Living With Family Despite Improved Job Market," www.pewsocialtrends.org, July 29, 2015, p. 7.

2. Paul Taylor, *The Next America: Boomers, Millennials, and the Looming Generational Showdown* (Public Affairs, 2015), pp. 144–145.

3. "It's even more diverse if we look at ... those aged twenty-five to thirty-four, with people of color making up 47 percent of the younger working class": Tamara Draut, *Sleeping Giant: How the New Working Class Will Transform America* (Anchor Books, 2016), p. 7; National Center for Education Statistics, *Digest of Education Statistics: 2017*, http://nces.ed.gov, Table 306.10.

4. William H. Frey, *Diversity Explosion: How New Racial Demographics are Remaking America* (Brookings Institution, 2015), pp. 169, 188.

5. James Tracy, *Dispatches Against Displacement: Field Notes From San Francisco's Housing Wars* (AK Press, 2014).

6. Taylor, *The Next America*, p. 11; Douglas S. Massey and Nancy A. Denton, *American Apartheid: Segregation and the Making of the Underclass* (Harvard University Press, 1993), pp. 84–88.

7. For example, 58 percent of families in the lowest quintile spend on average over half their earnings on rent; Jenny Schuetz, "Is the Rent 'Too Damn High'? Or are Incomes Too Low?," www.brookings.edu, December 19, 2017.

8. U.S. Bureau of Labor Statistics, "May 2017 National Occupational Employment and Wage Estimates United States": "Cross-Industry, Private Ownership Only," and "Federal, State, and Local Government, Including Government-Owned Schools and Hospitals and the U.S. Postal Service," www.bls.gov, March 30, 2018.

9. Federal Reserve Bank of St. Louis, "All Employees: Government, November 2017," https://fred.stlouisfed.org; Cato Institute, "Federal Spending by Agency, 1970–2017," www.downsizinggovernment.org.

10. NCES, *Digest of Education Statistics: 2017*, Table 503.20.

11. Completion rates improve by as much as 8 percent when individuals are traced, rather than setting specific "time-to-degree"

frameworks, such as 150 percent of normal time or a set number of years past the expected date of graduation: Frederick M. Hess, Mark Schneider, Kevin Carey, and Andrew P. Kelly, "Diplomas and Dropouts: Which Colleges Actually Graduate Their Students (and Which Don't)," www.aei.org, June 2009, p. 5; D. Shapiro, A. Dunbar, X. Yuan, A. Harrell, and P. K. Wakhungu, "Completing College: A National View of Student Attainment Rates – Fall 2008 Cohort," https://nscresearchcenter.org, November 2014, pp. 6, 12–13, 17.

12. NCES, *Digest of Education Statistics: 2017*, Tables 303.40, 303.55.

13. U.S. Bureau of Labor Statistics, "Occupations With The Most Job Growth, 2016–26," www.bls.gov, Table 1.4, April 11, 2018; Table 6, December 8, 2015.

14. Lawrence Mishel, Josh Bivens, Elise Gould, and Heidi Shierholz, *The State of Working America*, twelfth edition (Cornell University Press, 2012), pp. 306–308; Anthony P. Carnevale, Nicole Smith, and Jeff Strohl, "Help Wanted: Projections of Jobs and Education Requirements Through 2018," https://cew.georgetown.edu, June 2010, p. 14; Sandy Baum, Charles Kurose, and Jennifer Ma, "How College Shapes Lives: Understanding the Issues," http://trends.collegeboard.org, October 2013, pp. 37–40.

15. NCES, *Digest of Education Statistics: 2017*, Table 318.10; Michael Mandel, "An Analysis of Job and Wage Growth in the Tech/Telecom Sector," www.progressivepolicy.org, September 2017, p. 5.

16. Data USA, "Demographics: Detailed Occupation"; "Electricians," "Pipelayers, Plumbers, Pipefitters, & Steamfitters," "Police Officers," "Firefighters," https://datausa.io; Ginger Adams Otis, *Firefight: The Century-Long Battle to Integrate New York's Bravest* (St. Martin's Press, 2015).

17. Susan Chira and Catrin Einhorn, "How Tough Is It to Change a Culture of Harassment? Ask Women at Ford," *New York Times*, December 19, 2017; Susan Chira, "We Asked Women in Blue-Collar Workplaces About Harassment. Here Are Their Stories," *New York Times*, December 29, 2017.

18. Anthony P. Carnevale, Jeff Strohl, Ban Cheah, and Neil Ridley, "Good Jobs that Pay without a BA," https://goodjobsdata.org, 2017, pp. 1, 5.
19. Paul Beaudry, David A. Green, and Benjamin M. Sand, "The Great Reversal in the Demand for Skill and Cognitive Skills," *Journal of Labor Economics*, 34.1 (January 2016): 202; Jaison R. Abel and Richard Deitz, "Working as a Barista After College Is Not as Common as You Might Think," http://libertystreeteconomics. newyorkfed.org, January 11, 2016.
20. *National Association of Law Placement Bulletin*, September 2018, www.nalp.org.
21. Bryan College: https://www.bryan.edu.
22. U.S. Office of Personnel Management, "Historical Federal Workforce Tables: Executive Branch Civilian Employment Since 1940," www.opm.gov; U.S. Bureau of Labor Statistics, "All Employees, Thousands, Government, Seasonally Adjusted," https://beta.bls.gov, July 2, 2018.
23. Hironao Okahana and Enyu Zhou, "Graduate Enrollment and Degrees: 2006 to 2016," Council of Graduate Schools, www. cgsnet.org, October 2018, p. 30, Table B.9.
24. "Pursuing the American Dream: Economic Mobility Across Generations," www.pewtrusts.org, July 2012, p. 6; also, Chapter 2 of this text, Figures 2.1a and 2.1b.
25. See Chapter 2, Figure 2.2.
26. Guy Standing, *The Precariat: The New Dangerous Class* (Bloomsbury, 2011); Michael Hardt and Antonio Negri, *Multitude: War and Democracy in the Age of Empire* (Penguin, 2004).

Index

parental education, 14, 20–23, 32,
52
poverty, 112
private schools, 14, 31
upper-income families, 32–3, 54,
65, 126, 146n25
veterans, 74
China, 12
Civil Rights Movement, 111
Clapham, J. H., 4
class. *See also* gentrification.
changing nature of, 3, 16, 60, 70–1,
73–4, 76, 78–9, 89–90, 106
consciousness and identity, 7, 69,
73–4, 81, 82–3, 84, 85, 86–8,
89, 140
definitions of, 1–2, 18, 52, 56–60,
60–63, 82, 123, 136, 140, 141,
152n26, 152n28, 169n3
divisions and stratification, 7, 9,
13–14, 21, 23, 26, 31, 33, 34,
37, 50, 52–6, 57, 69, 122, 131
elusiveness of, 38, 56–60
race, and, 9–10, 11
Clinton administration, 111
Cobb, Jonathan, 82
college premium, 20, 106–9, 162n46
Collins, Randall, 81
commodities, 2, 4, 8, 12, 70, 78–9,
97, 113
communication skills, 100, 117
community colleges, students, and
degrees, 10, 19, *20 table 1.1*,
23–6, 27, *29 table 1.3*, *37 fig.
1.3*, 38, 49, 51, 59, 60, 61, 66,
67, 73, 76, 77, *101 table 4.1*,
102, 109, 135, 136, 145n15,
148n43, 149n5
consumption and mass consumption, 3, 62, 71, 78–82, 83

Corinthian Colleges, 67
creative arts, 39, 126, 137, 140
cutting-edge industries and
companies, 71–2, 108, 116

debt, 16, 48–51, 105, 125, 138. *See
also* student loans
deindustrialization, 6, 11, 17, 84,
94–5, 96, 104, 105, 106, 109,
122, 162n39
Democrats, 105
Department of Labor. *See* U.S.
Department of Labor
Depression. *See* Great Depression
diversity, 2, 13, 85, 119–23, 129,
169n3
downward mobility, 6, 7, 15, 17, 26,
44, 51–3, 61, 85, 108, 126,
135–6, 137, 138, 144n10
Draut, Tamar, 61

economic theory, 9, 16, 69, 107
economic reorganization, 7, 94, 97ff,
106
elite, 1, 15, 33–7, 48, 60, 65, 103,
111, 119, 123–8. *See also*
bourgeoisie, upper class.
colleges, schools, and institutions,
14, 28, 31, 32, 35, 36, 37, 64,
65, 71, 120
employment reorganization, 95–106
English language, 25, 62
enrollments college, 21, 25, 67,
73–4, *75 table 3.1*, 119, 120,
121–2, 133, 139, 166n30
equal opportunity programs, 33
Espenshade, Thomas J., 31–2, 36
ethnicity, 3, 10, 11, 13, 33, 34, 57, 84,
85, 106, 120, 121, 122, 130, 136
extracurricular activities, 32–3

factories and factory system, 4, 6,
95–6, 97, 104, 113, 136
faculty and professors, 27, 66, 74,
115, 121–2, 145n15, 167n36
family connections, 34, 136
family income, 7, 18, 19, 20–23, 31,
36, 49, 50, 52–4, 55, 89, 122,
144n7, 147n30
farming, 64, 65, 69, 77, 89, 103, *104
table 4.2*, 159n17
fast-food workers, 114–15
Federal Reserve Bank, 14, 39–40,
43, 46
Fed Ex, 116
financial aid, 42, 49, 51, 67, 68, 73,
149n4
first generation college students, 84
Fitzgerald, Scott, 61
Forbes (magazine), 127
for-profit and proprietary institutions, 14, 25, 51, 67, 68, 73, 116
four-year colleges, universities, and
institutions, 14, 19, 20–1, 23,
24, 25, 26–7, 30, 34, 35, 38, 40,
45, 49, 51, 61, 66, 67, 68, 76,
77, 107, 133, 145n15
Fraser, Steve, 70
Freeman, Richard, 5, 75, 91

gender, 3, 9–12, 34, 57, 85, 86, 106,
136
gentrification, 130–32
geography, 11–12, 13, 67, 84, 95
G.I. Bill (1944) (Servicemen's
Readjustment Act), 33, 73–5,
83
gig economy, 15, 48, 102, 116–19,
137
globalization, 97, 162n39
Gorz, André, 82, 85

governance, educational, 67
government funding and spending,
9, 16, 18, 27, 33, 49, 64–9,
72–3, 74, 76, 77, 78, 92, 96,
105, 110–12, 114, 115, 116,
122, 126, 132–3, 140, 141
government intervention, 105, 116
graduate school and graduate
education, 25, 49, 50–51, 121,
138
graduation rates, undergraduate, 8,
23, *26 table 1.2*, 34–5, 42, 68,
133, 149n5, 160n23
Great Depression (1930s), 72, 80,
83
Great Recession (2007–08), 16, 40,
92, 113–14, 124
gross domestic product (GDP), 105,
119, 135

Harrison, Bennett, 95
Head Start program, 33
Hecker, Daniel, 98
high school graduates and diplomas,
10, 19, 20, *20 table 1.1*, 21, 25,
27, 28, 30, *37 fig. 1.3*, 38, 41,
42, *58 fig. 2.3*, 58, 59, *59 fig.
2.4*, 61, 71, 72, 88, 92, 98, 102,
106, 107, 108, 109, 129,
148n43, 152n29, 160n23
home care workers, 115
home ownership, 16, 61, 81, 83, 124,
126
Hong Kong, 11
households, multi-generational, 129
Hout, Michael, 88
humanities, 45, 65

identity, and politics of, 1, 5, 14, 81,
82, 83, 84, 85, 86, 88, 89

re-industrialization, 94–7, 104
religion, 10, 34, 65, 84, 111
Republicans, 105

SAT (Scholastic Aptitude Test), 28,
 36
Say, Jean-Baptiste and Say's Law,
 109
self-employed, freelancers, and
 independent contractors, 89,
 97, 116, 118, 136, 166n27
Sennett, Richard, 82
service sectors and occupations, 7,
 17, 24–5, 43, 48, 63, 64, 70, 72,
 77–8, 77 table 3.2, 88, 89, 96,
 97–105, 104 table 4.2, 109, 111,
 114, 116, 161n30
 food services, 25, 43, 65, 72, 114,
 134, 137
 hospitality services, 108, 139
 personal services, 24, 31, 63, 99,
 113, 114, 134
 transportation services, 48, 63, 65,
 99, 114, 137
sexual orientation, 3, 10, 11, 57, 103
skilled work and workers, 6, 63, 71,
 73, 80–1, 89, 98, 101 table 4.1,
 104, 136
social darwinism, 33–4, 36–7
social sciences, 2, 45, 46 table 2.2, ,
 57, 65
socioeconomic background, 3, 16,
 29–33, 30 fig. 1.2, 34–35, 51,
 52, 62, 63, 122, 148n36
Spanish language, 62
Stanford University (CA), 13
state universities, 65
steel production and industry, 4, 75

STEM (science, technology,
 engineering, math) majors, 46
 table 2.3
stocks and stock market, 16, 72, 124,
 125, 127, 151n19
Strohl, Jeff, 60
student loans, 18, 48–51, 65, 68,
 126, 133, 150n16. See also debt
subsidies, government, 68, 69, 105,
 114–15, 116, 126, 133
Summers, Larry, 112–13

tax cuts, 16, 67, 133
Terkel, Studs, 85
tips, 114
tuition, 12, 31, 36, 49, 50, 64, 65, 68,
 73, 133, 147n30
Tunisia, 11
Turkey, 12
Twitter, 116, 117–18
two-year colleges. See community
 colleges.

Uber, 116
Uchitelle, Louis, 95
underemployment, 5, 11, 15, 17, 38,
 39–48, 49, 51, 52, 59, 60, 62, 63,
 75, 88, 90, 91–4, 98, 102, 106,
 107–8, 110, 111, 126, 134, 135,
 137, 138, 139, 149n1, 163n49
undergraduate education, cannibalization of, 138–9
underutilization, 92–4, 138
unemployment, 39, 44–7, 91, 92–3,
 111, 134, 138, 157n5
unions, 63, 70, 75, 98, 160n21
upper class, 1, 16, 31, 64, 78–9, 89,
 97, 124. See also bourgeoisie,
 elite.
upper middle class, 87, 123, 126